For Those We Love But See No Longer

For Those We Love But See No Longer

Daily Offices for Times of Grief

The Rev. Lisa Belcher Hamilton

Library of Congress Cataloging-in-Publication Data

Hamilton, Lisa Belcher, 1959–
For those we love but see no longer : Daily Offices for times of grief / Lisa Belcher Hamilton.
p. cm.
Includes bibliographical references.
ISBN 1-55725-271-8 (pbk.)
1. Bereavement—Prayer-books and devotions—English. 2. Consolation—Prayer-books and devotions—English. I. Title.
BV4905.2 .H355 2001
242'.4—dc21
00-012923

10 9 8 7 6 5 4 3

ISBN: 978-1-55725-271-5

Published by Paraclete Press
Brewster, Massachusetts
www.paracletepress.com

Printed in the United States of America.

For Scott Lane Hamilton
(1959–1991)
A man of God who pursued righteousness,
godliness, faith, love, endurance, gentleness.

Fight the good fight of faith;
take hold of the eternal life, to which you were called
and for which you made the good confession.

I Timothy 6:12 (NRSV)

Table of Contents

Acknowledgments

The making of any book represents the love of many people. This one is no exception. The love I felt as a small child, cuddled in the lap of my language-loving maternal gradmother, Effie Alice Hert Jackson, is here. The love of my own child, Edward Lane Hamilton, whose understanding of the world and of his mother staggers her, is here as well.

To the following contributors of ideas and criticism, I owe a special thanks: The Rev. Jamie Callaway, Dr. Peter Hawkins, Dr. Elizabeth Koenig, Sister Mary Michael, SSM, Alice Mindrum, The Rev. Fred Rogers, Robert Owens Scott, The Rev. Janna Tull Steed, and Sarah Watson Lovejoy and her family.

I am also especially appreciative of Phyllis Tickle, who believed enough in me to introduce me to her friends and colleagues at Paraclete Press, now mine as well: Dr. Lillian Miao and Sr. Mercy Minor.

I deeply appreciate the friends whose love did not end with Scott's death. You kept me from ending, and you and the friends with whom God has blessed me since make me glad indeed.

I am indebted to many, seen and unseen, living and dead, who have prayed this project to fruition. To God, I owe the most of all. May the words of this book and the meditations of our hearts be pleasing to our Creator, Redeemer, and Sustainer.

Preface

Our son was 26 months old the perfect June night he discovered lightning bugs. I can't count the times I've tried to bring back the conversation his Dada and I were having when he interrupted us to pry open his chubby fingers and see the bug glow green, then stop, then glow green again. "Look Dada, see bug light!" Teddy squealed, and with every ounce of his being, Scott helped him into his lap. They took turns holding the last gift Teddy gave his father.

When Scott had cancer, Teddy was forever giving him things—even his precious "yanyee," his much-snuggled blue blanket. When there was nothing on hand, Teddy "made" things. The morning of a chemotherapy treatment, we walked our dog to the park, where Teddy interrupted his climbing long enough to make and feed Scott pretend oatmeal. But nothing anyone could give him cured the cancer. It took death.

Death came the night Teddy discovered lightning bugs. Scott passed out as he tried to climb the stairs in our "starter house," and I dragged him to the bed crying, "I won't let you fall, I won't let you fall, I won't let you fall." I jabbered and prayed aloud until he opened his eyes and croaked out, "I love you." He even regained enough strength to say Compline with me. We kissed goodnight, and in the morning, we were still holding hands, but his was dead.

Everything was different that morning, including the way God was speaking to me in Psalm 91—the Psalm we always chose at Compline. Psalm 91 was one of the ways God broke through the cancer to teach us to pray together. Psalm 91, with its images of safety under God's wings, of refuge in angel's hands, promised us that there was no terror even in plague. It was the last psalm of Scott's life—and yet God did not "rescue him and bring him to honor." The last verse—"With long life will I satisfy him, and show him to salvation"—had once helped bring us the relief of sleep. Only after a few years of accusing God of betrayal did I come to realize that, for Scott, the psalm's promises are for eternity.

My being changed by the unchanging words of Psalm 91 is a discovery as ancient as the psalms themselves. Indeed, so is being changed by praying at fixed times of day. The psalms are often called "Jesus' prayers" because they were (and are) such an integral part of Jewish worship. Jews were expected to pray at fixed hours, and it's interesting to note how many important New Testament events occur at these times of prayer, as when Peter and John healed the lame man (Acts 3:1–10) who was lying at the "Beautiful gate" of the Temple; the apostles were entering for prayer at three in the afternoon.

Apparently it took some centuries for Christians to settle on a schedule of fixed prayer, with early writers advocating prayer three or five or seven times a day. All schedules, however, included prayer at sunrise and sunset. Today's Offices (the term comes from the Latin *opus Dei*, meaning "work of God") place us in communion with the earliest believers, as several elements (including the psalms and the Lord's Prayer) were used from the beginnings of our faith, although scriptural readings were not used in daily prayer, but saved for the Sunday Eucharist and other select occasions. By the mid-sixth century, the Daily Offices included Scripture, and due in large part to St. Benedict, were fixed in a shape that is familiar to Christians today. The seven Benedictine Hours are collapsed in the *The Book of Common Prayer* into Morning Prayer, Noontime Prayer, Vespers or Evening Prayer, and Compline, so the ancient structure and content connects not only with the living who pray them, but with the dead who have prayed them as well.

Perhaps grief has brought you to regulated prayer because you may find that structure helps you cope with the day. I did not return to work for some time after Scott's death, and I remember my relief at devising a schedule that ensured Teddy and I would be out of the house for a time every day. On Tuesdays, a plaster handprint recalls, we attended a "Mommy and Me" art class. I made certain that every day, we saw other people, even if they were strangers in the grocery store, and this was important. But the Daily Offices offer a holy connection to an unbroken chain of Christians—and provide us with deeper nourishment than we can devise alone.

When someone we love dies, it is often very painful to move to a new place. I remember the day of the Pittsburgh tag sale a year after Scott died because Teddy and I were moving to New Haven, where I would enter Divinity School. As I saw people carrying away things I'd sold them, I felt as if I were watching our life disappear down the driveway. I've never found it comfortable to move in any way—geographically, professionally, emotionally—and now, without Scott, I feel I am somehow being disloyal in moving. Saying familiar prayers in a familiar form is a security I can take from job to job, from home to home, from feeling to feeling, and the knowledge that Scott and I are linked in prayer has often brought me the feeling that he is proud of the moving I do.

Prayer is the most lasting way I know to cope with loneliness. In part, grief is lonely because there are so few people able to listen without wanting to "make it all better." One particularly bad day the summer Scott died, the phone rang, and when I said "Hello," I was greeted with, "You sound so much better. It's great that you're happy again." I spent the rest of the forgotten conversation staring at the front porch and wondering how I could sound better, and even happy, when the newspapers were piling up because I didn't have any interest in reading them.

Therapists would call my caller's comments "projection" —projecting onto me an image of what he wanted me to be. Projection is impossible in prayer, because prayer can offer a glimpse of ourselves and our lives through the eyes of God. In my experience, this level of prayer occurs most frequently when I am in the habit of praying so regularly that as the Rev. Suzanne Guthrie describes it, "Your soul becomes alert in anticipation, just as your stomach does if you eat at noon every day."[1] Committing yourself to regulated prayer in grief offers you a nourishing structure in difficult days and clears the way for a more honest knowledge of God, yourself, and your relationships with God and your loved one.

Fixed-time prayer offers us a larger purpose than learning to live with our own pain. As Phyllis Tickle describes it, "Like relay runners passing a lighted torch, those who do the work of fixed-hour prayer do create thereby a continuous cascade of praise before the throne of God."[2] The eight cancer months Scott and I shared, similar to our pregnancy months, were filled with purpose. The purpose was to poison the cancer, reverse the metastases, and pray a cure, ignoring the odds as stubbornly as we curled in hospital beds together, nursing Teddy as the chemotherapy dripped medical hope through Scott's body.

However difficult it was to realize that the purpose of prayer is to align oneself with God's will rather than hammer away on the merits of one's own desires, praying returned purpose to me. Imperceptibly, I began to pray for those beyond Scott, Teddy, and me. Prayer expands me still, as if I am a bowl being shaped by a potter. I am large enough to pray for a teenage friend in trouble, relatives I do not understand, people in car accidents—even when the accident is making me late for work. Prayer seems to welcome the stranger, so that reports from the morning news often find their way into noontime prayer.

I've worked on *For Those We Love But See No Longer* envisioning people silently praying on subways, because it was on New York's Lexington line that I first prayed intentionally, with the help of *Morning and Evening Prayer With Selected Psalms and Readings for the Church Year.*[3] I'm hopeful that *For Those We Love But See No Longer* can also used for praying aloud, in groups of people as well as alone. The good people at Paraclete have designed this book to be small enough to carry with you in purse or pocket, and with the help of the Good Paraclete, I hope it will provide you with a way to live days of grief. Praying at rising, noon, evening, and retiring with the Daily

Office links us to other Christians who engage in this common and ancient spiritual practice, and so we are less alone than we may feel. I've chosen readings and prayers for their purpose, variety, and faithfulness, and set them in the security and community of the Daily Offices as found in *The Book of Common Prayer.* Although this book is in no way intended to replace *The Book of Common Prayer*, it is nevertheless comforting to recall that Thomas Cranmer, chief architect of *The Book of Common Prayer*, began his work after losing his wife and their baby in childbirth.

I've selected Morning Prayer readings to help the griever face another day without those who are dead. Noonday readings are a cry of missing the dead, "whom we love but see no longer." Evening Prayer readings offer hope for the dead. At Compline, readings commend both oneself and the dead to God. Fridays are focused on God's grief at the crucifixion of Christ.

When used individually, the Office may be said silently or aloud. When used by a group, longer sections are divided so that each person or group takes turns. Lines to be read by the leader are followed by an asterisk (*). Group responses are indented and follow the asterisk.

All texts, including the Psalms, are excerpted from *The Book of Common Prayer* unless otherwise noted. Many of these texts have been adapted for this book. Such texts are indicated by the symbol †.

There is space for journaling at the end of each day, in the hope that your journaling can teach you about your grief—and therefore about yourself. You may want to write letters, to God, to your loved one, or even to yourself. Or perhaps writing prayers will feel more natural to you. At least sometimes, you may find yourself drawing. Whatever form or forms you use, dating your entries or even making an index will make your journaling more helpful to you over time.

Given that grief does not leave within seven days, you may wonder why *For Those We Love* provides only one week of Offices. First of all, I want this book to be portable: small enough to pray within a subway car. Second, I hope this will be a book you use as needed. There may be days or weeks at a time when your prayer feels more honest when you rely on the tried and true *Book of Common Prayer*, or when you utilize another form of prayer. To this end, I've recommended several books to which you may "graduate" or which you may wish to incorporate as supplementary even while using *For Those We Love*.

If you're familiar with the Daily Offices, you'll notice immediately that the Confession is missing from *For Those We Love But See No Longer*. If you feel that saying the Confession is helpful to you, by all means include it—the Rite II Confession from *The Book of Common Prayer* can be found at the end of this book.

My reason for excluding the Confession in *For Those We Love But See No Longer* is that Scott's death erupted a fireworks of guilt for me, and I suspect it may be common for a long period of time to need to pass before saying the Confession is helpful. Nevertheless, the Confession I so seldom said for so long was useful to me in bringing me closer to God through anger. Even now the Confession sometimes raises for me the question of whether God causes pain purposelessly. If God is omnipotent, isn't God culpable for cancer and all the pain it unleashes? Many times, I've said the Confession with my mouth while raging in my heart: "Who should be confessing to whom, God?" I've learned that times when my anger might be judged blasphemous seem to be used particularly well by God to deepen our relationship. As a wise friend of mine notes, "God doesn't cast us off because of our anger." Thank God.

When Scott was very ill, I faced a priest across our backyard picnic table and asked, "Is this happening because God *can't* stop it or because God *won't* stop it?" Two divinity school degrees later, I'm still searching for the reason(s) suffering and God cohabit our lives. The intersection seems to be nowhere other than the cross. When you find yourself at the cross, I pray that

For Those We Love But See No Longer will help you to remember that as lonely as Golgotha is, it is not a place where we are alone. Jesus' arms were nailed in a posture of embrace on the cross, and they are spread for us in fixed welcome. May prayer help you embrace his welcome.

1 *Praying the Hours* (Cambridge, MA: Cowley Publications, 2000), p. 3.

2 *The Divine Hours: Prayers for Summertime* (New York: Doubleday, 2000), p. ix.

3 Compiled and Edited by Howard Galley, published by Church Publishing, Inc.—and among recommended prayer books found on pages 189-192.

Monday

Monday Morning Prayer

The Invitation to Worship

Out of the deep have I called unto thee, O Lord: * Lord, hear my voice.
The Lord is full of compassion and mercy: * Come, let us adore him.
Glory to the Father, and to the Son, and to the Holy Spirit: * as it was in the beginning, is now, and will be for ever. Amen.

Psalm 86:1–13

Bow down your ear, O LORD, and answer me, * for I am poor and in misery.
Keep watch over my life, for I am faithful; * save your servant who puts his trust in you.
Be merciful to me, O LORD, for you are my God; * I call upon you all the day long.
Gladden the soul of your servant, * for to you, O LORD, I lift up my soul.
For you, O LORD, are good and forgiving, * and great is your love toward all who call upon you.
Give ear, O LORD, to my prayer, * and attend to the voice of my supplications.
In the time of my trouble I will call upon you, * for you will answer me.
Among the gods there is none like you, O LORD, * nor anything like your works.

All nations you have made will come and worship you, O LORD, * and glorify your Name.
For you are great; you do wondrous things; * and you alone are God.
Teach me your way, O LORD, and I will walk in your truth; * knit my heart to you that I may fear your Name.
I will thank you, O LORD my God, with all my heart, * and glorify your Name for evermore.
For great is your love toward me; * you have delivered me from the nethermost Pit.
Glory to the Father, and to the Son, and to the Holy Spirit: * as it was in the beginning, is now, and will be for ever. Amen.

The Word

Then fixing his eyes on his disciples he said:
How blessed are you who are poor:
the kingdom of God is yours.
Blessed are you who are hungry now:
you shall have your fill.
Blessed are you who are weeping now:
you shall laugh.
LUKE 6:20–21 (NJB)

Thanks be to God.

Canticle

THE FIRST SONG OF ISAIAH, ISAIAH 12:2–5

Surely, it is God who saves me; * I will trust in him and not be afraid.
For the Lord is my stronghold and my sure defense, * and he will be my Savior.
Therefore you shall draw water with rejoicing * from the springs of salvation.
And on that day you shall say, * Give thanks to the Lord and call upon his Name;
Make his deeds known among the peoples; * see that they remember that his Name is exalted.
Sing the praises of the Lord, for he has done great things, * and this is known in all the world.†
Glory to the Father, and to the Son, and to the Holy Spirit: * as it was in the beginning, is now, and will be for ever. Amen.

The Apostles' Creed

I believe in God, the Father almighty,
creator of heaven and earth.
I believe in Jesus Christ, his only Son, our Lord.
He was conceived by the power of the Holy Spirit
and born of the Virgin Mary.
He suffered under Pontius Pilate,
was crucified, died, and was buried.
He descended to the dead.
On the third day he rose again.

He ascended into heaven,
and is seated at the right hand of the Father.
He will come again to judge the living and
the dead.
I believe in the Holy Spirit,
the holy catholic Church,
the communion of saints,
the forgiveness of sins,
the resurrection of the body,
and the life everlasting. Amen.

The Prayers

The Lord be with you.
And also with you.
Let us pray.

Our Father in heaven,
hallowed be your Name,
your kingdom come,
your will be done,
on earth as in heaven.
Give us today our daily bread.
Forgive us our sins
as we forgive those
who sin against us.
Save us from the time of trial,
and deliver us from evil.
For the kingdom, the power,
and the glory are yours,
now and for ever. Amen.

The Petitions

Show us your mercy, O Lord; * And grant us your salvation.
Clothe your ministers with righteousness; * Let your people sing with joy.
Give peace, O Lord, in all the world; * For only in you can we live in safety.
Lord, keep this nation under your care; * And guide us in the way of justice and truth.
Let your way be known upon earth; * Your saving health among all nations.
Let not the needy, O Lord, be forgotten; * Nor the hope of the poor be taken away.
Create in us clean hearts, O God; * And sustain us with your Holy Spirit.

For our *brother/sister N.*, let us pray to our Lord Jesus Christ who said, "I am Resurrection, and I am Life."

Lord, you consoled Martha and Mary in their distress; draw near to us who mourn for *N.*, and dry the tears of those who weep.

Hear us, Lord.

You wept at the grave of Lazarus, your friend; comfort us in our sorrow.

Hear us, Lord.

You raised the dead to life; give to our *brother/sister* eternal life.

Hear us, Lord.

You promised paradise to the thief who repented; bring our *sister/brother* to the joys of heaven.

Hear us, Lord.

Our *brother/sister* was washed in Baptism and anointed with the Holy Spirit; give *him/her* fellowship with all your saints.

Hear us, Lord.

S/he was nourished with your Body and Blood; grant *her/him* a place at the table in your heavenly kingdom.

Hear us, Lord.

Comfort us in our sorrows at the death of *N.*; let our faith be our consolation, and eternal life our hope.†

Silence may follow.

The Collect

Grant, O Lord, to all who are bereaved the spirit of faith and courage, that *we* may have strength to meet the day to come with steadfastness and patience; not sorrowing without hope, but in remembrance of your great goodness, and in the expectation of eternal life with those *we* love. And this *we* ask in the Name of Jesus Christ our Savior. Amen.†

The Meditation

This may be read aloud by one person and followed by silence, or read by all present silently.

Well blest is he who has a dear one dead;
A friend whose face will never change—
A dear communion that will not grow strange;
The anchor of love is death.[4]

JOHN BOYLE O'REILLY

Free intercessions and/or reflections may be offered.

The Reflection

Is there blessing in your loss? Do you feel your loved one blessing you?

The Conclusion

Let us bless the Lord.
Thanks be to God.

Keep alert, stand firm in your faith, be courageous, be strong. Let all that you do be done in love. Amen.

I CORINTHIANS 16:13–14 (NRSV)

Monday Noonday Prayer

The Invitation to Worship

Take courage, my children, cry to God. * And he will deliver you from the power and hand of the enemy.

Glory to the Father, and to the Son, and to the Holy Spirit: * as it was in the beginning, is now, and will be for ever. Amen.

Psalm 121

I lift up my eyes to the hills; * from where is my help to come?
My help comes from the LORD, * the maker of heaven and earth.
He will not let your foot be moved * and he who watches over you will not fall asleep.
Behold, he who keeps watch over Israel * shall neither slumber nor sleep;
The LORD himself watches over you; * the LORD is your shade at your right hand,
So that the sun shall not strike you by day, * nor the moon by night.
The LORD shall preserve you from all evil; * it is he who shall keep you safe.
The LORD shall watch over your going out and your coming in, * from this time forth for evermore.
Glory to the Father, and to the Son, and to the Holy Spirit: * as it was in the beginning, is now, and will be for ever. Amen.

The Word

Simon Peter asked him, "Lord, where are you going?" Jesus replied, "Where I am going, you cannot follow now, but you will follow later."

JOHN 13:36 (NIV)

Thanks be to God.

The Meditation

This may be read aloud by one person and followed by silence, or read by all present silently.

According to II Samuel chapters 12–18, King David fathered many children. One of his sons, Absalom, killed another son, Amnon, because Amnon had raped their sister, Tamar. Absalom went into hiding, and "the soul of King David longed to go forth unto Absalom" (13:39). Still, when David's general Joab tricked the king into allowing Absalom to go home to Jerusalem, "the king said, 'Let him turn to his own house and let him not see my face.' . . . So Absalom dwelt two full years in Jerusalem and saw not the king's face" (14:24, 28). Absalom, treating Joab badly in the process, persisted: "Now therefore let me see the king's face; and if there be any iniquity in me, let him kill me. . . . And when he had called for Absalom, he came to the king, and bowed himself on his face to the ground before the king: and the king kissed Absalom" (14:32–33).

Still, Absalom's anger had festered, and he began to plot the overthrow of his father. Charismatic and handsome, with especially beautiful long, thick hair, Absalom was a talented politician. "Absalom said moreover, 'Oh that I were made judge in the land, that every man which hath any suit or cause might come unto me, and I would do him justice!' And it was so, that when any man came nigh to him to do him obeisance, he put forth his hand, and took it and kissed him. And on this manner did Absalom to all Israel that came to the king for judgment: so Absalom stole the hearts of the men of Israel" (15:4–6).

When the battle between the armies of the king and Absalom the usurper began, David said, "Deal gently for my sake with the young man, even with Absalom. And all the people heard. . . . And Absalom met the servants of David. And Absalom rode upon a mule, and the mule went under the thick boughs of a great oak, and his head caught hold of the oak and he was taken up between the heaven and the earth: and the mule that was under him went away" (18:5, 9).

As Absalom hung by his hair, imprisoned in the oak's branches, Joab drove three spears into the upstart's chest and ordered that the body be flung into a pit and covered with stones.

"And the king was much moved, and went up to the chamber over the gate, and wept: and as he went, thus he said, 'O my son Absalom, my son, my son, Absalom! Would God I had died for thee, O Absalom, my son, my son!'" (18:33) (KJV).

The Prayers

Lord, have mercy.
Christ, have mercy.
Lord, have mercy.

Our Father in heaven,
hallowed be your Name,
your kingdom come,
your will be done,
on earth as in heaven.
Give us today our daily bread.
Forgive us our sins
as we forgive those
who sin against us.
Save us from the time of trial,
and deliver us from evil.
For the kingdom, the power,
and the glory are yours,
now and for ever. Amen.

The Collect

O God of grace and glory, *we* remember before you this day *our* brother (sister) *N.* We thank you for giving *her/him* to *us*, to know and to love as a companion on *our* earthly pilgrimage. In your boundless compassion, console *us* who mourn. Give *us* faith to see in death the gate of eternal life, so that in quiet confidence *we* may continue *our* course on earth, until, by your call, we are reunited with those who have gone before; through Jesus Christ our Lord. Amen.†

Free intercessions and/or reflections may be offered.

The Reflection

In what ways has God responded to you in your loss? When have you felt God has not responded to your cry?

The Conclusion

Let us bless the Lord.
Thanks be to God.

Rest eternal grant to *N.*, O Lord,
And let light perpetual shine upon *him/her.*

Monday Evening Prayer

The Invitation to Worship

I am the Resurrection and I am the Life, says the Lord, * Whoever has faith in me shall have life, even though he die.
For if we have life, we are alive in the Lord, * And if we die, we die in the Lord.
So, then, whether we live or die, * We are the Lord's possession.†

O Gracious Light

O gracious Light,
pure brightness of the everliving Father in heaven,
O Jesus Christ, holy and blessed!
Now as we come to the setting of the sun,
and our eyes behold the vesper light,
we sing your praises, O God: Father, Son, and Holy Spirit.†

Psalm 107:1–9

Give thanks to the LORD, for he is good, * and his mercy endures for ever.
Let all those whom the LORD has redeemed proclaim * that he redeemed them from the hand of the foe.
He gathered them out of the lands; * from the east and from the west, from the north and from the south.
Some wandered in desert wastes; * they found no way to a city where they might dwell.
They were hungry and thirsty; * their spirits languished within them.
Then they cried to the LORD in their trouble, * and he delivered them from their distress.
He put their feet on a straight path * to go to a city where they might dwell.
Let them give thanks to the LORD for his mercy * and the wonders he does for his children.
For he satisfies the thirsty * and fills the hungry with good things.

Glory to the Father, and to the Son, and to the Holy Spirit: * as it was in the beginning, is now, and will be for ever. Amen.

The Word

For now we see through a glass, darkly;
but then face to face.
Now I know in part
but then I shall know all:
even as I am known.

I CORINTHIANS 13:12 (KJV)

Thanks be to God.

Canticle

THE SONG OF MARY, LUKE 1:46–55

My soul proclaims the greatness of the Lord, my spirit rejoices in God my Savior; * for he has looked with favor on his lowly servant.
From this day all generations will call me blessed: * the Almighty has done great things for me, and holy is his Name.
He has mercy on those who fear him * in every generation.
He has shown the strength of his arm, * he has scattered the proud in their conceit.
He has cast down the mighty from their thrones, * and has lifted up the lowly.
He has filled the hungry with good things, * and the rich he has sent away empty.

He has come to the help of his servant Israel, *
  for he has remembered his promise of mercy,
The promise he made to our fathers, * to
  Abraham and his children for ever.
Glory to the Father, and to the Son, and to the
  Holy Spirit: * as it was in the beginning, is
  now, and will be for ever. Amen.

The Apostles' Creed

I believe in God, the Father almighty,
  creator of heaven and earth.
I believe in Jesus Christ, his only Son, our Lord.
  He was conceived by the power of the
  Holy Spirit
  and born of the Virgin Mary.
  He suffered under Pontius Pilate,
  was crucified, died, and was buried.
  He descended to the dead.
  On the third day he rose again.
  He ascended into heaven,
  and is seated at the right hand of the Father.
  He will come again to judge the living and
  the dead.
I believe in the Holy Spirit,
  the holy catholic Church,
  the communion of saints,
  the forgiveness of sins,
  the resurrection of the body,
  and the life everlasting. Amen.

The Prayers

The Lord be with you.
And also with you.
Let us pray.

Our Father in heaven,
hallowed be your Name,
your kingdom come,
your will be done,
on earth as in heaven.
Give us today our daily bread.
Forgive us our sins
as we forgive those
who sin against us.
Save us from the time of trial,
and deliver us from evil.
For the kingdom, the power,
and the glory are yours,
now and for ever. Amen.

The Petition

Show us your mercy, O Lord; * And grant us your salvation.
Clothe your ministers with righteousness; * Let your people sing with joy.
Give peace, O Lord, in all the world; * For only in you can we live in safety.
Lord, keep this nation under your care; * And guide us in the way of justice and truth.

Let your way be known upon earth; * Your
saving health among all nations.
Let not the needy, O Lord, be forgotten; *
Nor the hope of the poor be taken away.
Create in us clean hearts, O God; * And
sustain us with your Holy Spirit.

The Collect

God of all, *we* pray to you for *N.*, and for all those whom *we* love but see no longer. Grant to them your peace; let light perpetual shine upon them; and, in your loving wisdom and almighty power, work in them the good purpose of your perfect will, through Jesus Christ our Lord. Amen.†

The Meditation

This may be read aloud by one person and followed by silence, or read by all present silently.

What is essential is invisible to the eye.[5]
ANTOINE DE SAINT-EXUPERY

Free intercessions and/or reflections may be offered.

The Reflection

How do you "see" those you've lost? How do you think they see you from the clearer vantage point of heaven?

The Conclusion

Let us bless the Lord.
Thanks be to God.

May the God of hope fill you with all joy and peace in believing . . . through the power of the Holy Spirit. Amen.
ROMANS 15:13 (NRSV)

Monday Compline

The Invitation to Worship

The Lord Almighty grant us a peaceful night and a perfect end. Amen.

Answer me when I call, O God, defender of my cause; * you set me free when I am hard-pressed; have mercy on me and hear my prayer.
Glory to the Father, and to the Son, and to the Holy Spirit: * as it was in the beginning, is now, and will be for ever. Amen.

Psalm 74:8–22

There are no signs for us to see; there is no prophet left; * there is not one among us who knows how long.
How long, O God, will the adversary scoff? * will the enemy blaspheme your Name for ever?

Why do you draw back your hand? * why is your right hand hidden in your bosom?
Yet God is my King from ancient times, * victorious in the midst of the earth.
You divided the sea by your might * and shattered the heads of the dragons upon the waters;
You crushed the heads of Leviathan * and gave him to the people of the desert for food.
You split open spring and torrent; * you dried up ever-flowing rivers.
Yours is the day, yours also the night; * you established the moon and the sun.
You fixed all the boundaries of the earth; * you made both summer and winter.
Remember, O LORD, how the enemy scoffed, * how a foolish people despised your Name.
Do not hand over the life of your dove to wild beasts; * never forget the lives of your poor.
Look upon your covenant; * the dark places of the earth are haunts of violence.
Let not the oppressed turn away ashamed; * let the poor and needy praise your Name.
Arise, O God, maintain your cause; * remember how fools revile you all day long.
Forget not the clamor of your adversaries, * the unending tumult of those who rise up against you.
Glory to the Father, and to the Son, and to the Holy Spirit: * as it was in the beginning, is now, and will be for ever. Amen.

The Word

He reveals the deep things of darkness and
brings deep shadows into the light.
JOB 12:22 (NIV)

Thanks be to God.

The Meditation

This may be read aloud by one person and followed by silence, or read by all present silently.

In You, therefore, O Lord God, I place my whole hope and refuge; on You I rest in my tribulations and anguish, for I find all is weak and unstable, no matter what it is, unless it is in You.

For many friends cannot profit me, nor can strong helpers assist, nor wise counselors give profitable answers, nor can the books of the learned yield any comfort, and no precious substance can deliver, nor can any place, however remote and lovely, give shelter, unless You Yourself assist, help, strengthen, console, instruct, and guard me.[6]

THOMAS À KEMPIS

The Prayers

Into your hands, O Lord, we commend our spirits; * For you have redeemed us, O Lord, O God of truth.
Keep us, O Lord, as the apple of your eye; * Hide us under the shadow of your wings.†

Lord, have mercy.
Christ, have mercy.
Lord, have mercy.

Our Father in heaven,
hallowed be your Name,
your kingdom come,
your will be done,
on earth as in heaven.
Give us today our daily bread.
Forgive us our sins
as we forgive those
who sin against us.
Save us from the time of trial,
and deliver us from evil.

Lord, hear our prayer;
And let our cry come to you.
Let us pray.

Keep watch, dear Lord, with those who work, or watch, or weep this night, and give your angels charge over those who sleep. Tend the sick, Lord Christ; give rest to the weary, bless the dying, soothe the suffering, pity the afflicted, shield the joyous; and all for your love's sake. Amen.

Free intercessions and/or reflections may be offered.

The Reflection

Job's friends gave him unsatisfactory advice, and ultimately he found solace in acknowledging that God is powerful, powerful enough to turn darkness into light. Perhaps Thomas à Kempis had the same experience in the fifteenth century! What helps you discern whether advice is of God? Perhaps using à Kempis's words will help. Take the advice to God and meditate on whether the advice is aiding God in assisting, helping, strengthening, consoling, instructing, and guarding you.

The Conclusion

Lord, you now have set your servant free * to go in peace as you have promised;
For these eyes of mine have seen the Savior, * whom you have prepared for all the world to see:
A Light to enlighten the nations, * and the glory of your people Israel.
Glory to the Father, and to the Son, and to the Holy Spirit: * as it was in the beginning, is now, and will be for ever. Amen.

Guide us waking, O Lord, and guard us sleeping; that awake we may watch with Christ, and asleep we may rest in peace.

Let us bless the Lord.
   Thanks be to God.

The almighty and merciful Lord, Father, Son, and Holy Spirit, bless us and keep us. Amen.

Thoughts & Memories

Tuesday

Tuesday Morning Prayer

The Invitation to Worship

Out of the deep have I called unto thee, O Lord: * Lord, hear my voice.
The Lord is full of compassion and mercy: * Come, let us adore him.
Glory to the Father, and to the Son, and to the Holy Spirit: * as it was in the beginning, is now, and will be for ever. Amen.

Psalm 61:1–5

Hear my cry, O God, * and listen to my prayer.
I call upon you from the ends of the earth with heaviness in my heart; * set me upon the rock that is higher than I.
For you have been my refuge, * a strong tower against the enemy.
I will dwell in your house for ever; * I will take refuge under the cover of your wings.
For you, O God, have heard my vows; * you have granted me the heritage of those who fear your Name.
Glory to the Father, and to the Son, and to the Holy Spirit: * as it was in the beginning, is now, and will be for ever. Amen.

The Word

"Do not let your hearts be troubled.
You trust in God, trust also in me.
In my Father's house there are many places to live in; otherwise I would have told you.
I am going now to prepare a place for you,
and after I have gone and prepared you a place,
I shall return to take you to myself,
so that you may be with me where I am."
JOHN 14:1–3 (NJB)

Thanks be to God.

Canticle

THE THIRD SONG OF ISAIAH, ISAIAH 60:1–3, 11A, 14C, 18–19

Arise, shine, for your light has come, * and the glory of the Lord has dawned upon you.
For behold, darkness covers the land; * deep gloom enshrouds the peoples.
But over you the Lord will rise, * and his glory will appear upon you.
Nations will stream to your light, * and kings to the brightness of your dawning.
Your gates will always be open; * by day or night they will never be shut.
They will call you The City of the Lord, * The Zion of the Holy One of Israel.
Violence will no more be heard in your land, * ruin or destruction within your borders.
You will call your walls, Salvation, * and all your portals, Praise.

The sun will no more be your light by day; *
by night you will not need the brightness of the moon.
The Lord will be your everlasting light, * and your God will be your glory.
Glory to the Father, and to the Son, and to the Holy Spirit: * as it was in the beginning, is now, and will be for ever. Amen.

The Apostles' Creed

I believe in God, the Father almighty,
creator of heaven and earth.
I believe in Jesus Christ, his only Son, our Lord.
He was conceived by the power of the Holy Spirit
and born of the Virgin Mary.
He suffered under Pontius Pilate,
was crucified, died, and was buried.
He descended to the dead.
On the third day he rose again.
He ascended into heaven,
and is seated at the right hand of the Father.
He will come again to judge the living and the dead.
I believe in the Holy Spirit,
the holy catholic Church,
the communion of saints,
the forgiveness of sins,
the resurrection of the body,
and the life everlasting. Amen.

The Prayers

The Lord be with you.
  And also with you.
Let us pray.

Our Father in heaven,
  hallowed be your Name,
  your kingdom come,
  your will be done,
  on earth as in heaven.
Give us today our daily bread.
Forgive us our sins
  as we forgive those
  who sin against us.
Save us from the time of trial,
  and deliver us from evil.
For the kingdom, the power,
  and the glory are yours,
  now and for ever. Amen.

The Petitions

Save your people, Lord, and bless your inheritance; * Govern and uphold them, now and always.
Day by day we bless you; * We praise your Name for ever.
Lord, keep us from all sin today; * Have mercy on us; Lord, have mercy.
Lord, show us your love and mercy; * For we put our trust in you.

In you, Lord, is our hope; * And we shall never
hope in vain.

For our *brother/sister N.*, let us pray to our Lord Jesus Christ who said, "I am Resurrection, and I am Life."

Lord, you consoled Martha and Mary in their distress; draw near to us who mourn for *N.*, and dry the tears of those who weep.

Hear us, Lord.

You wept at the grave of Lazarus, your friend; comfort us in our sorrow.

Hear us, Lord.

You raised the dead to life; give to our *brother/sister* eternal life.

Hear us, Lord.

You promised paradise to the thief who repented; bring our *sister/brother* to the joys of heaven.

Hear us, Lord.

Our *brother/sister* was washed in Baptism and anointed with the Holy Spirit; give *him/her* fellowship with all your saints.

Hear us, Lord.

S/he was nourished with your Body and Blood; grant *her/him* a place at the table in your heavenly kingdom.

Hear us, Lord.

Comfort us in our sorrows at the death of *N.*; let our faith be our consolation, and eternal life our hope.†

Silence may follow.

The Collect

Grant, O Lord, to all who are bereaved the spirit of faith and courage, that *we* may have strength to meet the day to come with steadfastness and patience; not sorrowing without hope, but in remembrance of your great goodness, and in the expectation of eternal life with those *we* love. And this *we* ask in the Name of Jesus Christ our Savior. Amen.†

The Meditation

This may be read aloud by one person and followed by silence, or read by all present silently.

These words: You will not be overcome, were said very insistently and strongly [by Jesus], for certainty and strength against every tribulation which may come. He did not say, "You will not be assailed, you will not be belabored, you will not be disquieted," but he said, "You will not be overcome."[7]

JULIAN OF NORWICH

Free intercessions and/or reflections may be offered.

The Reflection

At the age of 30½, Julian of Norwich was thought to be on her deathbed. In actuality, she was experiencing some of the most vivid visions of the suffering and risen Christ ever recorded. Julian received her visions while the plague, or Black Death, was striking down many people in its vicious path. Her visions, which gave her courage to live in conversation with God, included the image of God as close as our clothing and the image of God's love as common as the hazelnuts that carpeted the part of England where she lived.

This morning's psalm and Gospel speak of God and Jesus preparing homes for us, on earth and in heaven.

What kinds of images has your suffering brought? Have your images of God and images of your relationship with God changed in your grief?

The Conclusion

Let us bless the Lord.
   Thanks be to God.

Keep alert, stand firm in your faith, be courageous, be strong. Let all that you do be done in love. Amen.

1 CORINTHIANS 16:13–14 (NRSV)

Tuesday Noonday Prayer

The Invitation to Worship

Take courage, my children, cry to God. * And he will deliver you from the power and hand of the enemy.
Glory to the Father, and to the Son, and to the Holy Spirit: * as it was in the beginning, is now, and will be for ever. Amen.

Psalm 42

As the deer longs for the water-brooks, * so longs my soul for you, O God.
My soul is athirst for God, athirst for the living God; * when shall I come to appear before the presence of God?
My tears have been my food day and night, * while all day long they say to me, "Where now is your God?"
I pour out my soul when I think on these things: * how I went with the multitude and led them into the house of God,
With the voice of praise and thanksgiving, * among those who keep holy-day.
Why are you so full of heaviness, O my soul? * and why are you so disquieted within me?
Put your trust in God; * for I will yet give thanks to him, who is the help of my countenance, and my God.

My soul is heavy within me; * therefore I will remember you from the land of Jordan, and from the peak of Mizar among the heights of Hermon.

One deep calls to another in the noise of your cataracts; * all your rapids and floods have gone over me.

The Lord grants his loving-kindness in the daytime; * in the night season his song is with me, a prayer to the God of my life.

I will say to the God of my strength, "Why have you forgotten me? * and why do I go so heavily while the enemy oppresses me?"

While my bones are being broken, * my enemies mock me to my face;

All day long they mock me * and say to me, "Where now is your God?"

Why are you so full of heaviness, O my soul? * and why are you so disquieted within me?

Put your trust in God; * for I will yet give thanks to him, who is the help of my countenance, and my God.

Glory to the Father, and to the Son, and to the Holy Spirit: * as it was in the beginning, is now, and will be for ever. Amen.

The Word

The LORD is good to those whose hope is in him, to the one who seeks him; it is good to wait quietly for the salvation of the LORD.

LAMENTATIONS 3:25–26 (NIV)

Thanks be to God.

The Meditation

This may be read aloud by one person and followed by silence, or read by all present silently.

Nothing can make up for the absence of someone whom we love, and it would be wrong to try to find a substitute; we must simply hold out and see it through. That sounds very hard at first, but at the same time it is a great consolation, for the gap, as long as it remains unfilled, preserves the bonds between us. It is nonsense to say that God fills the gap; He doesn't fill it, but on the contrary, He keeps it empty and so helps us to keep alive our former communion with each other, even at the cost of pain.[8]

DIETRICH BONHOEFFER

The Prayers

Lord, have mercy.
Christ, have mercy.
Lord, have mercy.

Our Father in heaven,
hallowed be your Name,
your kingdom come,
your will be done,
on earth as in heaven.
Give us today our daily bread.
Forgive us our sins

as we forgive those
who sin against us.
Save us from the time of trial,
and deliver us from evil.
For the kingdom, the power,
and the glory are yours,
now and for ever. Amen.

The Collect

O God of grace and glory, *we* remember before you this day *our* brother (sister) *N.* We thank you for giving *her/him* to *us*, to know and to love as a companion on *our* earthly pilgrimage. In your boundless compassion, console *us* who mourn. Give *us* faith to see in death the gate of eternal life, so that in quiet confidence *we* may continue *our* course on earth, until, by your call, *we* are reunited with those who have gone before; through Jesus Christ our Lord. Amen.†

Free intercessions and/or reflections may be offered.

The Reflection

Do you feel a "gap" between you and your loved one? Describe it to your loved one—and to God. Do you think your loved one feels a gap? If so, how do you imagine the gap feels to your loved one?

The Conclusion

Let us bless the Lord.
  Thanks be to God.

Rest eternal grant to *N.*, O Lord,
And let light perpetual shine upon *him/her.*

Tuesday Evening Prayer

The Invitation to Worship

I am the Resurrection and I am the Life, says
  the Lord; * Whoever has faith in me shall
  have life, even though he die.
For if we have life, we are alive in the Lord, *
  And if we die, we die in the Lord.
So, then, whether we live or die, * We are the
  Lord's possession.†

O Gracious Light

O gracious Light,
pure brightness of the everliving Father in heaven,
O Jesus Christ, holy and blessed!
Now as we come to the setting of the sun,
and our eyes behold the vesper light,
we sing your praises, O God: Father, Son, and
Holy Spirit.†

Psalm 27:1, 5–13, 17–18

The LORD is my light and my salvation; whom then shall I fear? * the LORD is the strength of my life; of whom then shall I be afraid?

One thing have I asked of the LORD; one thing I seek; * that I may dwell in the house of the LORD all the days of my life;

To behold the fair beauty of the LORD * and to seek him in his temple.

For in the day of trouble he shall keep me safe in his shelter; * he shall hide me in the secrecy of his dwelling and set me high upon a rock.

Even now he lifts up my head * above my enemies round about me.

Therefore I will offer in his dwelling an oblation with sounds of great gladness; * I will sing and make music to the LORD.

Hearken to my voice, O LORD, when I call; * have mercy on me and answer me.

You speak in my heart and say, "Seek my face." * Your face, LORD, will I seek.

Hide not your face from me, * nor turn away your servant in displeasure.

You have been my helper; cast me not away; * do not forsake me, O God of my salvation.

What if I had not believed that I should see the goodness of the LORD * in the land of the living!

O tarry and await the LORD's pleasure; be strong, and he shall comfort your heart; * wait patiently for the LORD.
Glory to the Father, and to the Son, and to the Holy Spirit: * as it was in the beginning, is now, and will be for ever. Amen.

The Word

Trust in the LORD forever, * for the Lord, the LORD, is the Rock eternal.
ISAIAH 26:4 (NIV)

Thanks be to God.

Canticle

THE SONG OF MARY, LUKE 1:46–55

My soul proclaims the greatness of the LORD, my spirit rejoices in God my Savior; * for he has looked with favor on his lowly servant.
From this day all generations will call me blessed: * the Almighty has done great things for me, and holy is his Name.
He has mercy on those who fear him * in every generation.
He has shown the strength of his arm, * he has scattered the proud in their conceit.
He has cast down the mighty from their thrones, * and has lifted up the lowly.
He has filled the hungry with good things, * and the rich he has sent away empty.

He has come to the help of his servant Israel, * for he has remembered his promise of mercy,
The promise he made to our fathers, * to Abraham and his children for ever.
Glory to the Father, and to the Son, and to the Holy Spirit: * as it was in the beginning, is now, and will be for ever. Amen.

The Apostles' Creed

I believe in God, the Father almighty,
creator of heaven and earth.
I believe in Jesus Christ, his only Son, our Lord.
He was conceived by the power of the Holy Spirit
and born of the Virgin Mary.
He suffered under Pontius Pilate,
was crucified, died, and was buried.
He descended to the dead.
On the third day he rose again.
He ascended into heaven,
and is seated at the right hand of the Father.
He will come again to judge the living and the dead.
I believe in the Holy Spirit,
the holy catholic Church,
the communion of saints,
the forgiveness of sins,
the resurrection of the body,
and the life everlasting. Amen.

The Prayers

The Lord be with you.
And also with you.
Let us pray.

Our Father in heaven,
hallowed be your Name,
your kingdom come,
your will be done,
on earth as in heaven.
Give us today our daily bread.
Forgive us our sins
as we forgive those
who sin against us.
Save us from the time of trial,
and deliver us from evil.
For the kingdom, the power,
and the glory are yours,
now and for ever. Amen.

The Petition

Show us your mercy, O Lord; * And grant us your salvation.
Clothe your ministers with righteousness; * Let your people sing with joy.
Give peace, O Lord, in all the world; * For only in you can we live in safety.
Lord, keep this nation under your care; * And guide us in the way of justice and truth.
Let your way be known upon earth; * Your saving health among all nations.

Let not the needy, O Lord, be forgotten; *
Nor the hope of the poor be taken away.
Create in us clean hearts, O God; * And sustain us with your Holy Spirit.

The Collect

God of all, we pray to you for *N.*, and for all those whom we love but see no longer. Grant to them your peace; let light perpetual shine upon them; and, in your loving wisdom and almighty power, work in them the good purpose of your perfect will, through Christ our Lord. Amen.†

The Meditation

This may be read aloud by one person and followed by silence, or read by all present silently.

"Listen to the Right Voice."

Jesus Christ is the One we must listen to. As far as people are concerned, we ought to listen to them and believe them only insomuch as they are full of Jesus Christ's truth and authority. Books are good only to the extent that they teach us the good news of the gospel. Therefore, let us go straight to that sacred source.[9]

FRANÇOIS FÉNELON

Free intercessions and/or reflections may be offered.

The Reflection

Perhaps you find yourself receiving all kinds of advice, and wondering what of it to take and what of it to leave. This evening's psalm and Scripture give us the images of God as light and as a rock—very different images! What images of God help you turn to God as you discern advice you're given?

The Conclusion

Let us bless the Lord.
 Thanks be to God.

May the God of hope fill you with all joy and peace in believing . . . through the power of the Holy Spirit. Amen.
ROMANS 15:13 (NRSV)

Tuesday Compline

The Invitation to Worship

The Lord Almighty grant us a peaceful night and a perfect end. Amen.

Answer me when I call, O God, defender of my cause; * you set me free when I am hard-pressed; have mercy on me and hear my prayer.

Glory to the Father, and to the Son, and to the Holy Spirit: * as it was in the beginning, is now, and will be for ever. Amen.

Psalm 18:1–4, 6–7, 10–20

I love you, O LORD my strength, * O LORD my stronghold, my crag, and my haven.
My God, my rock in whom I put my trust, * my shield, the horn of my salvation, and my refuge; you are worthy of praise.
I will call upon the LORD, * and so shall I be saved from my enemies.
The breakers of death rolled over me, * and the torrents of oblivion made me afraid.
I called upon the LORD in my distress * and cried out to my God for help.
He heard my voice from his heavenly dwelling; * my cry of anguish came to his ears.
He parted the heavens and came down * with a storm cloud under his feet.
He mounted on cherubim and flew; * he swooped on the wings of the wind.
He wrapped darkness about him; * he made dark waters and thick clouds his pavilion.
From the brightness of his presence, through the clouds, * burst hailstones and coals of fire.
The LORD thundered out of heaven; * the Most High uttered his voice.

He loosed his arrows and scattered them; * he hurled thunderbolts and routed them.
The beds of the seas were uncovered, and the foundations of the world laid bare, * at your battle cry, O LORD, at the blast of the breath of your nostrils.
He reached down from on high and grasped me; * he drew me out of great waters.
He delivered me from my strong enemies
and from those who hated me; * for they were too mighty for me.
They confronted me in the day of my disaster; * but the LORD was my support.
He brought me out into an open place; * he rescued me because he delighted in me.
Glory to the Father, and to the Son, and to the Holy Spirit: * as it was in the beginning, is now, and will be for ever. Amen.

The Word

Who shall separate us from the love of Christ?
Neither death, nor life, nor angels, nor principalities, nor powers, nor things present, nor things to come,
Nor height, nor depth, nor any other creature, shall be able to separate us from the love of God, which is in Christ our Lord.*

ROMANS 8:35, 38–39 (KJV)

Thanks be to God.

The Meditation

This may be read aloud by one person and followed by silence, or read by all present silently.

Love is little
Love is low.
Love will make
My spirit grow.
Grow in peace,
Grow in light,
Love will do
The thing that's right.

TRADITIONAL SHAKER HYMN

The Prayers

Into your hands, O Lord, we commend our spirits; * For you have redeemed us, O Lord, O God of truth.
Keep us, O Lord, as the apple of your eye; * Hide us under the shadow of your wings.†

Lord, have mercy.
Christ, have mercy.
Lord, have mercy.

Our Father in heaven,
hallowed be your Name,
your kingdom come,
your will be done,
on earth as in heaven.
Give us today our daily bread.

Forgive us our sins
as we forgive those
who sin against us.
Save us from the time of trial,
and deliver us from evil.

Lord, hear our prayer;
And let our cry come to you.
Let us pray.

Keep watch, dear Lord, with those who work, or watch, or weep this night, and give your angels charge over those who sleep. Tend the sick, Lord Christ; give rest to the weary, bless the dying, soothe the suffering, pity the afflicted, shield the joyous; and all for your love's sake. Amen.

Free intercessions and/or reflections may be offered.

The Reflection

According to Paul, love is strong, yet the Shaker hymn describes love as gentle. And the psalmist portrays God loving through righteous anger. What is your grief teaching you about love?

The Conclusion

Lord, you now have set your servant free * to
go in peace as you have promised;

For these eyes of mine have seen the Savior, *
whom you have prepared for all the world
to see:
A Light to enlighten the nations, * and the
glory of your people Israel.
Glory to the Father, and to the Son, and to the
Holy Spirit: * as it was in the beginning, is
now, and will be forever. Amen.

Guide us waking, O Lord, and guard us sleeping; that awake we may watch with Christ, and asleep we may rest in peace.

Let us bless the Lord.
Thanks be to God.

The almighty and merciful Lord, Father, Son, and Holy Spirit, bless us and keep us.

Thoughts & Memories

Wednesday

Wednesday Morning Prayer

The Invitation to Worship

Out of the deep have I called unto thee, O Lord: * Lord, hear my voice.
The Lord is full of compassion and mercy: * Come, let us adore him.
Glory to the Father, and to the Son, and to the Holy Spirit: * as it was in the beginning, is now, and will be for ever. Amen.

Psalm 46

God is our refuge and strength, * a very present help in trouble.
Therefore we will not fear, though the earth be moved, * and though the mountains be toppled into the depths of the sea;
Though its waters rage and foam, * and though the mountains tremble at its tumult.
The LORD of hosts is with us; * the God of Jacob is our stronghold.
There is a river whose streams make glad the city of God, * the holy habitation of the Most High.
God is in the midst of her; she shall not be overthrown; * God shall help her at the break of day.
The nations make much ado, and the kingdoms are shaken; * God has spoken, and the earth shall melt away.

The LORD of hosts is with us; * the God of Jacob is our stronghold.

Come now and look upon the works of the LORD, * what awesome things he has done on earth.

It is he who makes war to cease in all the world; * he breaks the bow, and shatters the spear, and burns the shields with fire.

"Be still, then, and know that I am God; * I will be exalted among the nations; I will be exalted in the earth."

The LORD of hosts is with us; * the God of Jacob is our stronghold.

Glory to the Father, and to the Son, and to the Holy Spirit: * as it was in the beginning, is now, and will be for ever. Amen.

The Word

On this mountain the LORD Almighty will prepare a feast of rich food for all peoples, a banquet of aged wine—
the best of meats and the finest of wines.

On this mountain he will destroy
the shroud that enfolds all peoples,
the sheet that covers all nations;
he will swallow up death forever.

The Sovereign LORD will wipe away the tears from all faces;
he will remove the disgrace of his people

from all the earth.
The LORD has spoken.

In that day they will say,
"Surely this is our God;
we trusted in him, and he saved us.

This is the LORD, we trusted in him;
let us rejoice and be glad in his salvation."
ISAIAH 25:6–9 (NIV)

Thanks be to God.

Canticle

PRAYER OF MANASSEH, 1–2, 4, 6–7, 14

O Lord and Ruler of the hosts of heaven, *
God of Abraham, Isaac, and Jacob, and of all their righteous offspring:
You made the heavens and the earth, * with all their vast array.
All things quake with fear at your presence; *
they tremble because of your power.
But your merciful promise is beyond all measure; * it surpasses all that our minds can fathom.
O Lord, you are full of compassion, *
long-suffering, and abounding in mercy.
You will save me in accordance with your great mercy. Amen.
Glory to the Father, and to the Son, and to the Holy Spirit: * as it was in the beginning, is now, and will be for ever. Amen.

The Apostles' Creed

I believe in God, the Father almighty,
creator of heaven and earth.
I believe in Jesus Christ, his only Son, our Lord.
He was conceived by the power of the Holy Spirit
and born of the Virgin Mary.
He suffered under Pontius Pilate,
was crucified, died, and was buried.
He descended to the dead.
On the third day he rose again.
He ascended into heaven,
and is seated at the right hand of the Father.
He will come again to judge the living and the dead.
I believe in the Holy Spirit,
the holy catholic Church,
the communion of saints,
the forgiveness of sins,
the resurrection of the body,
and the life everlasting. Amen.

The Prayers

The Lord be with you.
And also with you.
Let us pray.

Our Father in heaven,
hallowed be your Name,
your kingdom come,

your will be done,
on earth as in heaven.
Give us today our daily bread.
Forgive us our sins
as we forgive those
who sin against us.
Save us from the time of trial,
and deliver us from evil.
For the kingdom, the power,
and the glory are yours,
now and for ever. Amen.

The Petitions

Show us your mercy, O Lord; * And grant us your salvation.
Clothe your ministers with righteousness; * Let your people sing with joy.
Give peace, O Lord, in all the world; * For only in you can we live in safety.
Lord, keep this nation under your care; * And guide us in the way of justice and truth.
Let your way be known upon earth; * Your saving health among all nations.
Let not the needy, O Lord, be forgotten; * Nor the hope of the poor be taken away.
Create in us clean hearts, O God; * And sustain us with your Holy Spirit.

For our *brother/sister* N., let us pray to our Lord Jesus Christ who said, "I am Resurrection, and I am Life."

Lord, you consoled Martha and Mary in their distress; draw near to us who mourn for *N.*, and dry the tears of those who weep.

Hear us, Lord.

You wept at the grave of Lazarus, your friend; comfort us in our sorrow.

Hear us, Lord.

You raised the dead to life; give to our *brother/sister* eternal life.

Hear us, Lord.

You promised paradise to the thief who repented; bring our *sister/brother* to the joys of heaven.

Hear us, Lord.

Our *brother/sister* was washed in Baptism and anointed with the Holy Spirit; give *him/her* fellowship with all your saints.

Hear us, Lord.

S/he was nourished with your Body and Blood; grant *her/him* a place at the table in your heavenly kingdom.

Hear us, Lord.

Comfort us in our sorrows at the death of *N.*; let our faith be our consolation, and eternal life our hope.†

Silence may follow.

The Collect

Grant, O Lord, to all who are bereaved the spirit of faith and courage, that *we* may have strength to meet the day to come with steadfastness and patience; not sorrowing without hope, but in remembrance of your great goodness, and in the expectation of eternal life with those *we* love. And this *we* ask in the Name of Jesus Christ our Savior. Amen.†

The Meditation

This may be read aloud by one person and followed by silence, or read by all present silently.

"O Grief"

O who will give me tears? Come all you springs,
Dwell in my head and eyes; come clouds and rain:
My grief needs all the watery things
That nature has produced. Let every vein
Suck up a river to supply my eyes,
My weary weeping eyes too dry for me,
Unless they get new conduits, new supplies
To bear them out, and with my state agree.
What are two shallow fords, two little spouts
Of a less world? The greater is but small,
A narrow cupboard for my griefs and doubts,
Which lack provision in the midst of all.

Verses, you are too fine a thing, too wise
For my rough sorrows; cease, be dumb and mute,
Give up your feet and running to my eyes,
And keep your measures for some lover's lute,
Whose grief allows him music and a rhyme:
For mine excludes both measure, tune, and time.
Alas, my God![10]

GEORGE HERBERT

Free intercessions and/or reflections may be offered.

The Reflection

What do your tears mean? What purposes do your tears have? What do you think about the tears of Jesus, who wept when he was told Lazarus was dead?

The Conclusion

Let us bless the Lord.
Thanks be to God.

Keep alert, stand firm in your faith, be courageous, be strong. Let all that you do be done in love. Amen.

1 CORINTHIANS 16:13–14 (NRSV)

Wednesday Noonday Prayer

The Invitation to Worship

Take courage, my children, cry to God. * And he will deliver you from the power and hand of the enemy.
Glory to the Father, and to the Son, and to the Holy Spirit: * as it was in the beginning, is now, and will be for ever. Amen.

Psalm 119: 169–176

Let my cry come before you, O LORD; * give me understanding, according to your word.
Let my supplication come before you; * deliver me, according to your promise.
My lips shall pour forth your praise, * when you teach me your statutes.
My tongue shall sing of your promise, * for all your commandments are righteous.
Let your hand be ready to help me, * for I have chosen your commandments.
I long for your salvation, O LORD, * and your law is my delight.
Let me live, and I will praise you, * and let your judgments help me.
I have gone astray like a sheep that is lost; * search for your servant, for I do not forget your commandments.
Glory to the Father, and to the Son, and to the

Holy Spirit: * as it was in the beginning, is now, and will be for ever. Amen.

The Word

There is always hope for a tree:
when felled, it can start its life again;
its shoots continue to sprout.

Its roots may have grown old in the earth,
its stump rotting in the ground,
but let it scent the water, and it buds,
and puts out branches like a plant newly set.

Can the dead come back to life?
Day after day of my service, I should be waiting for my relief to come.

Then you would call, and I should answer,
you would want to see once more what you have made.

JOB 14:7–9, 14–15 (NJB)

Thanks be to God.

The Meditation

This may be read aloud by one person and followed by silence, or read by all present silently.

Oh, only for so short a while have you loaned us to each other, because we take form in your act of drawing us, and we take life in your painting us, and we breathe in your singing us.

But only for so short a while have you loaned us to each other.

TRADITIONAL AZTEC PRAYER

The Prayers

Lord, have mercy.
  Christ, have mercy.
Lord, have mercy.

Our Father in heaven,
  hallowed be your Name,
  your kingdom come,
  your will be done,
  on earth as in heaven.
Give us today our daily bread.
Forgive us our sins
  as we forgive those
  who sin against us.
Save us from the time of trial,
  and deliver us from evil.
For the kingdom, the power,
  and the glory are yours,
  now and for ever. Amen.

The Collect

O God of grace and glory, *we* remember before you this day *our* brother (sister) *N.* We thank you for giving *her/him* to *us*, to know and to love as a companion on *our* earthly pilgrimage.

In your boundless compassion, console *us* who mourn. Give *us* faith to see in death the gate of eternal life, so that in quiet confidence *we* may continue our course on earth, until, by your call, *we* are reunited with those who have gone before; through Jesus Christ our Lord. Amen.†

Free intercessions and/or reflections may be offered.

The Reflection

This noon's Scripture is from Job's "despondent prayer." Later, he proclaims, "I know that my redeemer liveth, and that he shall stand at the latter day upon the earth: And though after my skin worms destroy this body, yet in my flesh shall I see God." (19:25–26, KJV). How do you think his outlook was transformed? In what ways are you changing in the midst of your suffering?

The Conclusion

Let us bless the Lord.
  Thanks be to God.

Rest eternal grant to *N.*, O Lord,
And let light perpetual shine upon *him/her*.

Wednesday Evening Prayer

The Invitation to Worship

I am the Resurrection, and I am the Life, says the Lord; * Whoever has faith in me shall have life, even though he die.
For if we have life, we are alive in the Lord, * And if we die, we die in the Lord.
So, then, whether we live or die, * We are the Lord's possession.†

O Gracious Light

O gracious Light,
pure brightness of the everliving Father in heaven,
O Jesus Christ, holy and blessed!
Now as we come to the setting of the sun,
and our eyes behold the vesper light,
we sing your praises, O God: Father, Son, and Holy Spirit.†

Psalm 116:1–15

I love the LORD, because he has heard the voice of my supplication, * because he has inclined his ear to me whenever I called upon him.
The cords of death entangled me; the grip of the grave took hold of me; * I came to grief and sorrow.
Then I called upon the Name of the LORD: *

"O LORD, I pray you, save my life."
Gracious is the LORD and righteous; * our God is full of compassion.
The LORD watches over the innocent; * I was brought very low, and he helped me.
Turn again to your rest, O my soul, * for the LORD has treated you well.
For you have rescued my life from death, * my eyes from tears, and my feet from stumbling.
I will walk in the presence of the LORD * in the land of the living.
I believed, even when I said, "I have been brought very low." * In my distress I said, "No one can be trusted."
How shall I repay the LORD * for all the good things he has done for me?
I will lift up the cup of salvation * and call upon the Name of the LORD.
I will fulfill my vows to the LORD * in the presence of all his people.
Precious in the sight of the LORD * is the death of his servants.
O LORD, I am your servant; * I am your servant and the child of your handmaid; you have freed me from my bonds.
I will offer you the sacrifice of thanksgiving * and call upon the Name of the LORD.
Glory to the Father, and to the Son, and to the Holy Spirit: * as it was in the beginning, is now, and will be for ever. Amen.

The Word

"Come to me, all you who labor and are overburdened, and I will give you rest.
Shoulder my yoke and learn from me, for I am gentle and humble in heart, *and you will find rest for your souls.*
Yes, my yoke is easy, and my burden light."
MATTHEW 11:28–30 (NJB)

Thanks be to God.

Canticle

THE SONG OF MARY, LUKE 1:46–55

My soul proclaims the greatness of the Lord, my spirit rejoices in God my Savior; * for he has looked with favor on his lowly servant.
From this day all generations will call me blessed: * the Almighty has done great things for me, and holy is his Name.
He has mercy on those who fear him * in every generation.
He has shown the strength of his arm, * he has scattered the proud in their conceit.
He has cast down the mighty from their thrones, * and has lifted up the lowly.
He has filled the hungry with good things, * and the rich he has sent away empty.
He has come to the help of his servant Israel, * for he has remembered his promise of mercy,

The promise he made to our fathers, * to
Abraham and his children for ever.
Glory to the Father, and to the Son, and to the
Holy Spirit: * as it was in the beginning, is
now, and will be for ever. Amen.

The Apostles' Creed

I believe in God, the Father almighty,
creator of heaven and earth.
I believe in Jesus Christ, his only Son, our Lord.
He was conceived by the power of the
Holy Spirit
and born of the Virgin Mary.
He suffered under Pontius Pilate,
was crucified, died, and was buried.
He descended to the dead.
On the third day he rose again.
He ascended into heaven,
and is seated at the right hand of the Father.
He will come again to judge the living and
the dead.
I believe in the Holy Spirit,
the holy catholic Church,
the communion of saints,
the forgiveness of sins,
the resurrection of the body,
and the life everlasting. Amen.

The Prayers

The Lord be with you.
  And also with you.
Let us pray.

Our Father in heaven,
  hallowed be your Name,
  your kingdom come,
  your will be done,
  on earth as in heaven.
Give us today our daily bread.
Forgive us our sins
  as we forgive those
  who sin against us.
Save us from the time of trial,
  and deliver us from evil.
For the kingdom, the power,
  and the glory are yours,
  now and for ever. Amen.

The Petition

Show us your mercy, O Lord; * And grant us
  your salvation.
Clothe your ministers with righteousness; * Let
  your people sing with joy.
Give peace, O Lord, in all the world; * For only
  in you can we live in safety.
Lord, keep this nation under your care; * And
  guide us in the way of justice and truth.

Let your way be known upon earth; * Your saving health among all nations.
Let not the needy, O Lord, be forgotten; * Nor the hope of the poor be taken away.
Create in us clean hearts, O God; * And sustain us with your Holy Spirit.

The Collect

God of all, we pray to you for *N.*, and for all those whom we love but see no longer. Grant to them your peace; let light perpetual shine upon them; and, in your loving wisdom and almighty power, work in them the good purpose of your perfect will, through Christ our Lord. Amen.†

The Meditation

This may be read aloud by one person and followed by silence, or read by all present silently.

The practice of the presence of God strengthens our hope. Our hope increases as our spiritual knowledge increases, as our faith lays hold the very secrets of God. By finding in God a beauty surpassing not only physical bodies on earth, but the beauty of the most perfect souls and of angels, our hope is strengthened.[11]

BROTHER LAWRENCE

Free intercessions and/or reflections may be offered.

The Reflection

Do you find obstacles when you try to rest in God? What does your hesitation tell you—and God? Do you think that practicing hope will help you grow in God? One way of practicing hope may be psalms such as tonight's, in which the psalmist is looking back at a hopeless time of grief and sorrow.

The Conclusion

Let us bless the Lord.
  Thanks be to God.

May the God of hope fill you with all joy and peace in believing . . . through the power of the Holy Spirit. Amen.
ROMANS 15:13 (NRSV)

Wednesday Compline

The Invitation to Worship

The Lord Almighty grant us a peaceful night and a perfect end. Amen.

Answer me when I call, O God, defender of my cause; * you set me free when I am hard-pressed; have mercy on me and hear my prayer.
Glory to the Father, and to the Son, and to the Holy Spirit: * as it was in the beginning, is now, and will be for ever. Amen.

Psalm 146:4–9

Happy are they who have the God of Jacob for their help! * whose hope is in the LORD their God;

Who made heaven and earth, the seas, and all that is in them; * who keeps his promise for ever;

Who gives justice to those who are oppressed, * and food to those who hunger.

The LORD sets the prisoners free; the LORD opens the eyes of the blind; * the LORD lifts up those who are bowed down;

The LORD loves the righteous; the LORD cares for the stranger; * he sustains the orphan and widow, but frustrates the way of the wicked.

The LORD shall reign for ever, * your God, O Zion, throughout all generations.

Glory to the Father, and to the Son, and to the Holy Spirit: * as it was in the beginning, is now, and will be for ever. Amen.

The Word

Jacob left Beer-sheba and set out for Haran. When he reached a certain place, he stopped for the night because the sun had set. Taking one of the stones there, he put it under his head and lay down to sleep.

He had a dream in which he saw a stairway resting on the earth, with its top reaching to heaven, and the angels of God were ascending and descending on it.

There above it stood the LORD, and he said, "I am the LORD, the God of your father Abraham and the God of Isaac. . . . I am with you and will watch over you wherever you go, and I will bring you back to this land. I will not leave you until I have done what I have promised you."

When Jacob awoke from his sleep, he thought, "Surely the LORD is in this place and I was not aware of it." He was afraid and said, "How awesome is this place! This is none other than the house of God; this is the gate of heaven."

GENESIS 28:10–13, 15–17 (NIV)

Thanks be to God.

The Meditation

This may be read aloud by one person and followed by silence, or read by all present silently.

Lord, it can be truly said that You cradle Your children asleep in Your arms during this long night of faith, and that You are pleased to allow an infinite variety of thoughts to pass through their minds—thoughts that are holy and full of mystery. In the state in which these dreams of the night place them, they do indeed experience terrible torments of fear, anguish, and weariness, but on the bright day of glory, You will make them disappear and turn into joy.[12]

REV. JEAN-PIERRE DE CAUSSADE, S.J.

The Prayers

Into your hands, O Lord, we commend our
  spirits; * For you have redeemed us, O Lord,
  O God of truth.
Keep us, O Lord, as the apple of your eye; *
  Hide us under the shadow of your wings.†

Lord, have mercy.
  Christ, have mercy.
Lord, have mercy.

Our Father in heaven,
  hallowed be your Name,
  your kingdom come,
  your will be done,
  on earth as in heaven.
Give us today our daily bread.
Forgive us our sins
  as we forgive those
  who sin against us.
Save us from the time of trial,
  and deliver us from evil.

Lord, hear our prayer;
  And let our cry come to you.
Let us pray.

Keep watch, dear Lord, with those who work, or watch, or weep this night, and give your angels charge over those who sleep. Tend the sick, Lord Christ; give rest to the weary, bless the dying, soothe the suffering, pity the afflicted, shield the joyous; and all for your love's sake. Amen.

Free intercessions and/or reflections may be offered.

The Reflection

What do your nights teach you? What are your dreams teaching you?

The Conclusion

Lord, you now have set your servant free * to
go in peace as you have promised;
For these eyes of mine have seen the Savior, *
whom you have prepared for all the world
to see:
A Light to enlighten the nations, * and the
glory of your people Israel.
Glory to the Father, and to the Son, and to the Holy Spirit: * as it was in the beginning, is now, and will be for ever. Amen.

Guide us waking, O Lord, and guard us sleeping; that awake we may watch with Christ, and asleep we may rest in peace.

Let us bless the Lord.
Thanks be to God.

The almighty and merciful Lord, Father, Son, and Holy Spirit, bless us and keep us.

Thoughts & Memories

Thursday

Thursday Morning Prayer

The Invitation to Worship

Out of the deep have I called unto thee, O Lord: * Lord, hear my voice.
The Lord is full of compassion and mercy: * Come, let us adore him.
Glory to the Father, and to the Son, and to the Holy Spirit: * as it was in the beginning, is now, and will be for ever. Amen.

Psalm 35

Fight those who fight me, O LORD; * attack those who are attacking me.
Take up shield and armor * and rise up to help me.
Draw the sword and bar the way against those who pursue me; * say to my soul, "I am your salvation."
Let those who seek after my life be shamed and humbled; * let those who plot my ruin fall back and be dismayed.
Let them be like chaff before the wind, * and let the angel of the LORD drive them away.
Let their way be dark and slippery, * and let the angel of the LORD pursue them.
For they have secretly spread a net for me without a cause; * without a cause they have dug a pit to take me alive.

Let ruin come upon them unawares; * let them be caught in the net they hid; let them fall into the pit they dug.

Then I will be joyful in the LORD; * I will glory in his victory.

My very bones will say, "LORD, who is like you? * You deliver the poor from those who are too strong for them, the poor and needy from those who rob them."

Malicious witnesses rise up against me; * they charge me with matters I know nothing about.

They pay me evil in exchange for good; * my soul is full of despair.

But when they were sick I dressed in sack-cloth * and humbled myself by fasting;

I prayed with my whole heart, as one would for a friend or a brother; * I behaved like one who mourns for his mother, bowed down and grieving.

But when I stumbled, they were glad and gathered together; they gathered against me; * strangers whom I did not know tore me to pieces and would not stop.

They put me to the test and mocked me; * they gnashed at me with their teeth.

O LORD, how long will you look on? * rescue me from the roaring beasts, and my life from the young lions.

I will give you thanks in the great congregation; * I will praise you in the mighty throng.

Do not let my treacherous foes rejoice over me, * nor let those who hate me without a cause wink at each other.
For they do not plan for peace, * but invent deceitful schemes against the quiet in the land.
They opened their mouths at me and said, * "Aha! we saw it with our own eyes."
You saw it, O LORD; do not be silent; * O Lord, be not far from me.
Awake, arise, to my cause! * to my defense, my God and my Lord!
Give me justice, O LORD my God, according to your righteousness; * do not let them triumph over me.
Do not let them say in their hearts, "Aha! just what we want!" * Do not let them say, "We have swallowed him up."
Let all who rejoice at my ruin be ashamed and disgraced; * let those who boast against me be clothed with dismay and shame.
Let those who favor my cause sing out with joy and be glad; * let them say always, "Great is the LORD, who desires the prosperity of his servant."
And my tongue shall be talking of your righteousness * and of your praise all the day long.
Glory to the Father, and to the Son, and to the Holy Spirit: * as it was in the beginning, is now, and will be for ever. Amen.

The Word

Jesus then went into the Temple and drove out all those who were selling and buying there; he upset the tables of the money-changers and the seats of the dove-sellers. He said to them, "According to scripture, '*my house shall be called a house of prayer,*' but you are turning it into a *bandits'* den."

MATTHEW 21:12–13 (NJB)

Thanks be to God.

Canticle

THE SECOND SONG OF ISAIAH, ISAIAH 55:6–11

Seek the LORD while he wills to be found; * call upon him when he draws near.
Let the wicked forsake their ways * and the evil ones their thoughts;
And let them turn to the LORD, and he will have compassion, * and to our God, for he will richly pardon.
For my thoughts are not your thoughts, * nor your ways my ways, says the LORD.
For as the heavens are higher than the earth, * so are my ways higher than your ways, and my thoughts than your thoughts.
For as rain and snow fall from the heavens * and return not again, but water the earth,
Bringing forth life and giving growth, * seed for sowing and bread for eating,

So is my word that goes forth from my mouth; *
it will not return to me empty;
But it will accomplish that which I have
purposed, * and prosper in that for which I
sent it.
Glory to the Father, and to the Son, and to the
Holy Spirit: * as it was in the beginning, is
now, and will be for ever. Amen.

The Apostles' Creed

I believe in God, the Father almighty,
creator of heaven and earth.
I believe in Jesus Christ, his only Son, our Lord.
He was conceived by the power of the
Holy Spirit
and born of the Virgin Mary.
He suffered under Pontius Pilate,
was crucified, died, and was buried.
He descended to the dead.
On the third day he rose again.
He ascended into heaven,
and is seated at the right hand of the Father.
He will come again to judge the living and
the dead.
I believe in the Holy Spirit,
the holy catholic Church,
the communion of saints,
the forgiveness of sins,
the resurrection of the body,
and the life everlasting. Amen.

The Prayers

The Lord be with you.
  And also with you.
Let us pray.

Our Father in heaven,
  hallowed be your Name,
  your kingdom come,
  your will be done,
  on earth as in heaven.
Give us today our daily bread.
Forgive us our sins
  as we forgive those
  who sin against us.
Save us from the time of trial,
  and deliver us from evil.
For the kingdom, the power,
  and the glory are yours,
  now and for ever. Amen.

The Petitions

Save your people, LORD, and bless your inheritance; * Govern and uphold them, now and always.
Day by day we bless you; * We praise your Name for ever.
LORD, keep us from all sin today; * Have mercy on us, LORD, have mercy.
LORD, show us your love and mercy; * For we put our trust in you.

In you, LORD, is our hope; * And we shall
never hope in vain.

For our *brother/sister N.*, let us pray to our Lord Jesus Christ who said, "I am Resurrection and I am Life."

Lord, you consoled Martha and Mary in their distress; draw near to us who mourn for *N.*, and dry the tears of those who weep.

Hear us, Lord.

You wept at the grave of Lazarus, your friend; comfort us in our sorrow.

Hear us, Lord.

You raised the dead to life; give to our *brother/sister* eternal life.

Hear us, Lord.

You promised paradise to the thief who repented; bring our *sister/brother* to the joys of heaven.

Hear us, Lord.

Our *brother/sister* was washed in Baptism and anointed with the Holy Spirit; give *him/her* fellowship with all your saints.

Hear us, Lord.

S/he was nourished with your Body and Blood; grant *her/him* a place at the table in your heavenly kingdom.

Hear us, Lord.

Comfort us in our sorrows at the death of *N.*; let our faith be our consolation, and eternal life our hope.†

Silence may follow.

The Collect

Grant, O Lord, to all who are bereaved the spirit of faith and courage, that *we* may have strength to meet the day to come with steadfastness and patience; not sorrowing without hope, but in remembrance of your great goodness, and in the expectation of eternal life with those *we* love. And this *we* ask in the Name of Jesus Christ our Savior. Amen.†

The Meditation
This may be read aloud by one person and followed by silence, or read by all present silently.

Meanwhile, where is God? This is one of the most disquieting symptoms. When you are happy, so happy that you have no sense of needing Him, so happy that you are tempted to feel His claims upon you as an interruption, if you remember yourself and turn to Him with gratitude and praise, you will be—or so it feels —welcomed with open arms. But go to Him when your need is desperate, when all other help is in vain, and what do you find? A door slammed in your face, and a sound of bolting and double bolting on the inside. After that, silence. You may as well turn away. The longer you wait, the more emphatic the silence will become. There are no lights in the windows. It might as well be an empty house. Was it ever inhabited? It seemed so once. And that seeming was as strong as this. What can this mean? Why is He so present a commander in our time of prosperity and so very absent a help in time of trouble?[13]

C.S. Lewis

Free intercessions and/or reflections may be offered.

The Reflection

You need look no further than the psalms to see that the Bible is full of angry people beloved by God. As this morning's readings demonstrate, Jesus felt angry and abandoned sometimes. Meditate on your anger—toward God, toward the living, toward the dead. And remember that God will not cast you out for feeling angry. In fact, bringing your anger to God may bring you closer to God.

The Conclusion

Let us bless the Lord.
Thanks be to God.

Keep alert, stand firm in your faith, be courageous, be strong. Let all that you do be done in love. Amen.

I CORINTHIANS 16:13–14 (NRSV)

Thursday Noonday Prayer

The Invitation to Worship

Take courage, my children, cry to God. * And he will deliver you from the power and hand of the enemy.

Glory to the Father, and to the Son, and to the Holy Spirit: * as it was in the beginning, is now, and will be for ever. Amen.

Psalm 57:1–3

Be merciful to me, O God, be merciful, for I have taken refuge in you; * in the shadow of your wings will I take refuge until this time of trouble has gone by.

I will call upon the Most High God, * the God who maintains my cause.

He will send from heaven and save me; * he will confound those who trample upon me;

God will send forth his love and his faithfulness.

Glory to the Father, and to the Son, and to the Holy Spirit: * as it was in the beginning, is now, and will be for ever. Amen.

The Word

My soul is bereft of peace;
I have forgotten what happiness is;

So I say, "Gone is my glory,
and all that I had hoped for
from the LORD."

The thought of my affliction and my homelessness,
is wormwood and gall!
My soul continually thinks of it
and is bowed down within me.

But this I call to mind,
and therefore I have hope:

The steadfast love of the LORD never ceases,
his mercies never come to an end;
they are new every morning;
great is your faithfulness.

"The LORD is my portion," says my soul,
"therefore I will hope in him."
The LORD is good to those who wait for him,
to the soul that seeks him;

For the LORD will not reject forever.
Although he causes grief,
he will have compassion,
according to the abundance of his steadfast
love;
for he does not willingly afflict
or grieve anyone.
LAMENTATIONS 3:17–25, 31–33 (NRSV)

Thanks be to God.

The Meditation

This may be read aloud by one person and followed by silence, or read by all present silently.

God does not cheapen himself or us by offering easy answers to the anguished *Why?* that we who are human cannot help but ask. The mystery of life and death and suffering remains a mystery in all human generations, and it is no less a mystery for us. We don't get a quick fix from our faith.[14]

EDMUND LEE BROWNING

The Prayers

Lord, have mercy.
Christ, have mercy.
Lord, have mercy.

Our Father in heaven,
hallowed be your Name,
your kingdom come,

your will be done,
on earth as in heaven.
Give us today our daily bread.
Forgive us our sins
as we forgive those
who sin against us.
Save us from the time of trial,
and deliver us from evil.
For the kingdom, the power,
and the glory are yours,
now and for ever. Amen.

The Collect

O God of grace and glory, *we* remember before you this day *our* brother (sister) *N.* We thank you for giving *her/him* to *us*, to know and to love as a companion on *our* earthly pilgrimage. In your boundless compassion, console *us* who mourn. Give *us* faith to see in death the gate of eternal life, so that in quiet confidence *we* may continue *our* course on earth, until, by your call, *we* are reunited with those who have gone before; through Jesus Christ our Lord. Amen.†

Free intercessions and/or reflections may be offered.

The Reflection

The Scripture for today claims that God "does not willingly afflict or grieve anyone." Have you ever asked the anguished "Why does suffering exist in the world?" If God is both all-powerful and all-loving?

The Conclusion

Let us bless the Lord.
Thanks be to God.

Rest eternal grant to *N.*, O Lord,
And let light perpetual shine upon *him/her.*

Thursday Evening Prayer

The Invitation to Worship

I am the Resurrection, and I am the Life, says the Lord; * Whoever has faith in me shall have life, even though he die.
For if we have life, we are alive in the Lord, * And if we die, we die in the Lord.
So, then, whether we live or die, * We are the Lord's possession.

O Gracious Light

O gracious Light,
pure brightness of the everliving Father in heaven,
O Jesus Christ, holy and blessed!
Now as we come to the setting of the sun,
and our eyes behold the vesper light,
we sing your praises, O God: Father, Son, and Holy Spirit.†

Psalm 23 (KJV)

The Lord is my shepherd; * I shall not want.
He maketh me to lie down in green pastures; *
he leadeth me beside the still waters.
He restoreth my soul; * he leadeth me in the paths of righteousness for his Name's sake.
Yea, though I walk through the valley of the shadow of death, I will fear no evil; * for thou art with me; thy rod and thy staff, they comfort me.
Thou preparest a table before me in the presence of mine enemies; * thou anointest my head with oil; my cup runneth over.
Surely goodness and mercy shall follow me all the days of my life, * and I will dwell in the house of the Lord for ever.
Glory to the Father, and to the Son, and to the Holy Spirit: * as it was in the beginning, is now, and will be for ever. Amen.

The Word

"I am the good shepherd: the good shepherd lays down his life for the sheep. The hired man, since he is not the shepherd and the sheep do not belong to him, abandons the sheep as soon as he sees a wolf coming, and runs away, and then the wolf attacks and scatters the sheep; he runs away because he is only a hired man and has no concern for his sheep.

"I am the good shepherd: I know my own and my own know me, just as the Father knows me and I know the Father; and I lay down my life for the sheep. And there are other sheep I have that are not of this fold, and I must lead these too. They too will listen to my voice, and there will be only one flock, one shepherd."
JOHN 10:11–16 (NJB)

Thanks be to God.

Canticle

THE SONG OF MARY, LUKE 1:46–55

My soul proclaims the greatness of the Lord,
my spirit rejoices in God my Savior; * for he has looked with favor on his lowly servant.
From this day all generations will call me blessed: * the Almighty has done great things for me, and holy is his Name.
He has mercy on those who fear him * in every generation.
He has shown the strength of his arm, * he has scattered the proud in their conceit.
He has cast down the mighty from their thrones, * and has lifted up the lowly.
He has filled the hungry with good things, * and the rich he has sent away empty.
He has come to the help of his servant Israel, * for he has remembered his promise of mercy,

The promise he made to our fathers, * to
Abraham and his children for ever.
Glory to the Father, and to the Son, and to the
Holy Spirit: * as it was in the beginning, is
now, and will be for ever. Amen.

The Apostles' Creed

I believe in God, the Father almighty,
creator of heaven and earth.
I believe in Jesus Christ, his only Son, our Lord.
He was conceived by the power of the
Holy Spirit
and born of the Virgin Mary.
He suffered under Pontius Pilate,
was crucified, died, and was buried.
He descended to the dead.
On the third day he rose again.
He ascended into heaven,
and is seated at the right hand of the Father.
He will come again to judge the living and
the dead.
I believe in the Holy Spirit,
the holy catholic Church,
the communion of saints,
the forgiveness of sins,
the resurrection of the body,
and the life everlasting. Amen.

The Prayers

The Lord be with you.
  And also with you.
Let us pray.

Our Father in heaven,
  hallowed be your Name,
  your kingdom come,
  your will be done,
  on earth as in heaven.
Give us today our daily bread.
Forgive us our sins
  as we forgive those
  who sin against us.
Save us from the time of trial,
  and deliver us from evil.
For the kingdom, the power,
  and the glory are yours,
  now and for ever. Amen.

The Petition

Show us your mercy, O Lord; * And grant us your salvation.
Clothe your ministers with righteousness; * Let your people sing with joy.
Give peace, O Lord, in all the world; * For only in you can we live in safety.
Lord, keep this nation under your care; * And guide us in the way of justice and truth.

Let your way be known upon earth; * Your
saving health among all nations.
Let not the needy, O Lord, be forgotten; *
Nor the hope of the poor be taken away.
Create in us clean hearts, O God; * And
sustain us with your Holy Spirit.

The Collect

God of all, *we* pray to you for *N.*, and for all those whom *we* love but see no longer. Grant to them your peace; let light perpetual shine upon them; and, in your loving wisdom and almighty power, work in them the good purpose of your perfect will, through Christ our Lord. Amen.†

The Meditation

This may be read aloud by one person and followed by silence, or read by all present silently.

Death is nothing at all. I have only slipped away into the next room. I am I and you are you. Whatever we were to each other, that we still are. Call me by my old familiar name, speak to me in the easy way which you always used. Put no difference in your tone, wear no forced air of solemnity or sorrow. Laugh as we always laughed at the little jokes we enjoyed together. Let my name be ever the household word that it always was, let it be spoken without effect, without the trace of a shadow on it.

Life means all that it ever meant. It is the same as it ever was; there is unbroken continuity. Why should I be out of mind because I am out of sight? I am waiting for you, for an interval, somewhere very near, just round the corner. All is well.[15]

HENRY SCOTT HOLLAND

Free intercessions and/or reflections may be offered.

The Reflection

When my husband died, I wanted to die too. It helped to have a little boy with soft baby skin who needed me, only me, to nurse him. It helped when a priest told me, "You belong here like the stars and the trees." It helped when I thought of Jesus between us, holding our hands. Maybe it will help you to read the 23rd Psalm while visualizing your loved ones and yourself belonging in the same fold, the flock of Christ. Know that Christ links the rooms of the living and the dead.

The Conclusion

Let us bless the Lord.
   Thanks be to God.

May the God of hope fill you with all joy and peace in believing . . . through the power of the Holy Spirit. Amen.
ROMANS 15:13 (NRSV)

Thursday Compline

The Invitation to Worship

The Lord Almighty grant us a peaceful night and a perfect end. Amen.

Answer me when I call, O God, defender of my cause; * you set me free when I am hard-pressed; have mercy on me and hear my prayer.
Glory to the Father, and to the Son, and to the Holy Spirit: * as it was in the beginning, is now, and will be forever. Amen.

Psalm 31:1–11, 14–16, 24

In you, O LORD, have I taken refuge; let me never be put to shame; * deliver me in your righteousness.
Incline your ear to me; * make haste to deliver me.
Be my strong rock, a castle to keep me safe, for you are my crag and my stronghold; * for the sake of your Name, lead me and guide me.
Take me out of the net that they have secretly set for me, * for you are my tower of strength.
Into your hands I commend my spirit, * for you have redeemed me, O LORD, O God of truth.

I hate those who cling to worthless idols, * and I put my trust in the LORD.
I will rejoice and be glad because of your mercy; * for you have seen my affliction; you know my distress.
You have not shut me up in the power of the enemy; * you have set my feet in an open place.
Have mercy on me, O LORD, for I am in trouble; * my eye is consumed with sorrow, and also my throat and my belly.
For my life is wasted with grief, and my years with sighing; * my strength fails me because of affliction, and my bones are consumed.
I have become a reproach to all my enemies and even to my neighbors, a dismay to those of my acquaintance; * when they see me in the street they avoid me.
But as for me, I have trusted in you, O LORD. * I have said, "You are my God.
My times are in your hand; * rescue me from the hand of my enemies, and from those who persecute me.
Make your face to shine upon your servant, * and in your loving-kindness save me."
Be strong and let your heart take courage, * all you who wait for the LORD.
Glory to the Father, and to the Son, and to the Holy Spirit: * as it was in the beginning, is now, and will be forever. Amen.

The Word

Now that very same day, two of them were on their way to a village called Emmaus, seven miles from Jerusalem, and they were talking together about all that had happened. And it happened that as they were talking together and discussing it, Jesus himself came up and walked by their side; but their eyes were prevented from recognizing him.
LUKE 24:13–16 (NJB)

The Word of the Lord.

The Meditation

This may be read aloud by one person and followed by silence, or read by all present silently.

"Lead, Kindly Light"

Lead, kindly Light, amid the encircling gloom;
Lead thou me on;
The night is dark, and I am far from home;
Lead thou me on;
Keep thou my feet; I do not ask to see
The distant scene; one step enough for me.

I was not ever thus, nor prayed that thou
Shouldst lead me on;
I loved to choose and see my path; but now
Lead thou me on;
I loved the garish day, and, spite of fears,
Pride ruled my will: remember not past years.

So long thy prayer hath blest me, sure it still
  Will lead me on
O'er moor and fen, o'er crag and torrent, till
  The night is gone;
And with the morn those angel faces smile
Which I have loved long since, and lost
  awhile.[16]

JOHN HENRY CARDINAL NEWMAN

The Prayers

Into your hands, O Lord, we commend our spirits; * For you have redeemed us, O Lord, O God of truth.
Keep us, O Lord, as the apple of your eye; * Hide us under the shadow of your wings.†

Lord, have mercy.
  Christ, have mercy.
Lord, have mercy.

Our Father in heaven,
  hallowed be your Name,
  your kingdom come,
  your will be done,
  on earth as in heaven.
Give us today our daily bread.
Forgive us our sins
  as we forgive those
  who sin against us.
Save us from the time of trial,
  and deliver us from evil.

Lord, hear our prayer;
And let our cry come to you.
Let us pray.

Keep watch, dear Lord, with those who work, or watch, or weep this night, and give your angels charge over those who sleep. Tend the sick, Lord Christ; give rest to the weary, bless the dying, soothe the suffering, pity the afflicted, shield the joyous; and all for your love's sake. Amen.

Free intercessions and/or reflections may be offered.

The Reflection

On the road to Emmaus, two of Jesus' followers didn't recognize their risen Lord. What keeps your eyes from recognizing God in your life? Can you remember times in the past when you felt God a kindly light leading you? To remember those times may make it easier for you, as the psalmist says, to put this time in God's hand and to know Christ's presence.

The Conclusion

Lord, you now have set your servant free * to
go in peace as you have promised;
For these eyes of mine have seen the Savior, *
whom you have prepared for all the world
to see:

Friday

Friday Morning Prayer

The Invitation to Worship

Out of the deep have I called unto thee, O Lord: * Lord, hear my voice.
The Lord is full of compassion and mercy: * Come, let us adore him.
Glory to the Father, and to the Son, and to the Holy Spirit: * as it was in the beginning, is now, and will be for ever. Amen.

Psalm 22:1–11

My God, my God, why have you forsaken me? * and are so far from my cry and from the words of my distress?
O my God, I cry in the daytime, but you do not answer; * by night as well, but I find no rest.
Yet you are the Holy One, * enthroned upon the praises of Israel.
Our forefathers put their trust in you; * they trusted, and you delivered them.
They cried out to you and were delivered; * they trusted in you and were not put to shame.
But as for me, I am a worm and no man, * scorned by all and despised by the people.
All who see me laugh me to scorn; * they curl their lips and wag their heads, saying,

"He trusted in the LORD; let him deliver him; * let him rescue him, if he delights in him."
Yet you are he who took me out of the womb, * and kept me safe upon my mother's breast.
I have been entrusted to you ever since I was born; * you were my God when I was still in my mother's womb.
Be not far from me, for trouble is near, * and there is none to help.
Glory to the Father, and to the Son, and to the Holy Spirit: * as it was in the beginning, is now, and will be for ever. Amen.

The Word

"My God, my God, why hast thou forsaken me?"

CHRIST ON THE CROSS, MATTHEW 27:46 (KJV)

The Word of the Lord.

Canticle

You are God: we praise you; * You are the Lord: we acclaim you; You are the eternal Father:
All creation worships you; * To you all angels, all the powers of heaven, Cherubim and Seraphim, sing in endless praise:
Holy, holy, holy Lord, God of power and might, * heaven and earth are full of your glory.

The glorious company of apostles praise you. *
The noble fellowship of prophets praise you.
The white-robed army of martyrs praise you.
Throughout the world the holy Church acclaims you; * Father, of majesty unbounded, your true and only Son, worthy of all worship, and the Holy Spirit, advocate and guide.
You, Christ, are the king of glory, * the eternal Son of the Father.
When you became man to set us free * you did not shun the Virgin's womb.
You overcame the sting of death * and opened the kingdom of heaven to all believers.
You are seated at God's right hand in glory. *
We believe that you will come and be our judge.
Come then, Lord, and help your people, bought with the price of your own blood, * and bring us with your saints to glory everlasting.
Glory to the Father, and to the Son, and to the Holy Spirit: * as it was in the beginning, is now, and will be for ever. Amen.

The Apostles' Creed

I believe in God, the Father almighty,
creator of heaven and earth.
I believe in Jesus Christ, his only Son, our Lord.
He was conceived by the power of the Holy Spirit

and born of the Virgin Mary.
He suffered under Pontius Pilate,
was crucified, died, and was buried.
He descended to the dead.
On the third day he rose again.
He ascended into heaven,
and is seated at the right hand of the Father.
He will come again to judge the living and the dead.
I believe in the Holy Spirit,
the holy catholic Church,
the communion of saints,
the forgiveness of sins,
the resurrection of the body,
and the life everlasting. Amen.

The Prayers

The Lord be with you.
And also with you.
Let us pray.

Our Father in heaven,
hallowed be your Name,
your kingdom come,
your will be done,
on earth as in heaven.
Give us today our daily bread.
Forgive us our sins
as we forgive those
who sin against us.

Save us from the time of trial,
and deliver us from evil.
For the kingdom, the power,
and the glory are yours,
now and for ever. Amen.

The Petitions

Show us your mercy, O Lord; * And grant us your salvation.
Clothe your ministers with righteousness; * Let your people sing with joy.
Give peace, O Lord, in all the world; * For only in you can we live in safety.
Lord, keep this nation under your care; * And guide us in the way of justice and truth.
Let your way be known upon earth; * Your saving health among all nations.
Let not the needy, O Lord, be forgotten; * Nor the hope of the poor be taken away.
Create in us clean hearts, O God; * And sustain us with your Holy Spirit.

For our *brother/sister N.*, let us pray to our Lord Jesus Christ who said, "I am Resurrection, and I am Life."

Lord, you consoled Martha and Mary in their distress; draw near to us who mourn for *N.*, and dry the tears of those who weep.

Hear us, Lord.

You wept at the grave of Lazarus, your friend; comfort us in our sorrow.

Hear us, Lord.

You raised the dead to life; give to our *brother/sister* eternal life.

Hear us, Lord.

You promised paradise to the thief who repented; bring our *sister/brother* to the joys of heaven.

Hear us, Lord.

Our *brother/sister* was washed in Baptism and anointed with the Holy Spirit; give *him/her* fellowship with all your saints.

Hear us, Lord.

S/he was nourished with your Body and Blood; grant *her/him* a place at the table in your heavenly kingdom.

Hear us, Lord.

Comfort us in our sorrows at the death of *N.*; let our faith be our consolation, and eternal life our hope.†

Silence may follow.

The Collect

Grant, O Lord, to all who are bereaved the spirit of faith and courage, that we may have strength to meet the day to come with steadfastness and patience; not sorrowing without hope, but in remembrance of your great goodness, and in the expectation of eternal life with those we love. And this we ask in the Name of Jesus Christ our Savior. Amen.†

The Meditation

This may be read aloud by one person and followed by silence, or read by all present silently.

From "For the Fallen"

They shall not grow old, as we that are left to grow old:
Age shall not weary them, nor the years condemn.
At the going down of the sun and in the morning,
We will remember them.[17]

LAURENCE BINYON

Free intercessions and/or reflections may be offered.

The Reflection

What kinds of feelings do Jesus' words "Why hast thou forsaken me?" bring up for you? Do you feel closer to Jesus, because you understand how he felt? Do you feel angry with God for forsaking Jesus, or for forsaking anyone else? Is remembering sometimes painful because of feeling forsaken?

The Conclusion

Let us bless the Lord.
Thanks be to God.

Keep alert, stand firm in your faith, be courageous, be strong. Let all that you do be done in love. Amen.
1 CORINTHIANS 16:13–14 (NRSV)

Friday Noonday Prayer

The Invitation to Worship

Take courage, my children, cry to God. * And he will deliver you from the power and hand of the enemy.
Glory to the Father, and to the Son, and to the Holy Spirit: * as it was in the beginning, is now, and will be for ever. Amen.

Psalm 22:11–18

Be not far from me, for trouble is near, * and there is none to help.
Many young bulls encircle me; * strong bulls of Bashan surround me.

They open wide their jaws at me, * like a ravening and a roaring lion. I am poured out like water;
all my bones are out of joint; * my heart within my breast is melting wax. My mouth is dried out like a pot-sherd;
my tongue sticks to the roof of my mouth; * and you have laid me in the dust of the grave.
Packs of dogs close me in, and gangs of evildoers circle around me; * they pierce my hands and my feet; I can count all my bones.
They stare and gloat over me; * they divide my garments among them; they cast lots for my clothing.
Be not far away, O Lord; * you are my strength; hasten to help me.
Glory to the Father, and to the Son, and to the Holy Spirit: * as it was in the beginning, is now, and will be for ever. Amen.

The Word

When the sixth hour [noon] came there was darkness over the whole land until the ninth hour. And at the ninth hour Jesus cried out in a loud voice, "Eloi, Eloi, lama sabachthani?" which means, *"My God, my God, why have you forsaken me?"* When some of those who stood by heard this, they said, "Listen, he is calling on Elijah." Someone ran and soaked a sponge in vinegar and, putting it on a reed, gave it to him to drink saying, "Wait! And see if Elijah will come to take him down." But Jesus gave a loud cry and breathed his last. And the veil of the Sanctuary was torn in two from top to bottom. The centurion, who was standing in front of him, had seen how he died, and he said, "In truth, this man was Son of God."

MARK 15:33–39 (NJB)

The Word of the Lord.

The Meditation

This may be read aloud by one person and followed by silence, or read by all present silently.

And I found comfort in weeping in your sight for her and for myself, in her behalf and my own. And I gave way to the tears I had been holding back, refreshing my heart with them, and it found rest in them, for it was in your ears, not in those of men who would have interpreted my weeping scornfully.[18]

AUGUSTINE OF HIPPO,
TO GOD ON THE DEATH OF HIS MOTHER

The Prayers

Lord, have mercy.
Christ, have mercy.
Lord, have mercy.

Our Father in heaven,
hallowed be your Name,
your kingdom come,
your will be done,
on earth as in heaven.
Give us today our daily bread.
Forgive us our sins
as we forgive those
who sin against us.
Save us from the time of trial,
and deliver us from evil.
For the kingdom, the power,
and the glory are yours,
now and for ever. Amen.

The Collect

O God of grace and glory, *we* remember before you this day our brother (sister) *N.* We thank you for giving *her/him* to *us*, to know and to love as a companion on *our* earthly pilgrimage. In your boundless compassion, console *us* who mourn. Give *us* faith to see in death the gate of eternal life, so that in quiet confidence *we* may continue *our* course on earth, until, by your call, *we* are reunited with those who have gone before; through Jesus Christ our Lord. Amen.†

Free intercessions and/or reflections may be offered.

The Reflection

What is it that you are crying out to God? Is your crying out to God's ears different from your crying out to human ears?

The Conclusion

Let us bless the Lord.
  Thanks be to God.

Rest eternal grant to *N.*, O Lord,
And let light perpetual shine upon *him/her.*

Friday Evening Prayer

The Invitation to Worship

I am the Resurrection, and I am the Life, says the Lord, * Whoever has faith in me shall have life, even though he die.
For if we have life, we are alive in the Lord, * and if we die, we die in the Lord.
So, then, whether we live or die, * We are the Lord's possession.†

O Gracious Light

O gracious Light,
pure brightness of the everliving Father in heaven,
O Jesus Christ, holy and blessed!

Now as we come to the setting of the sun,
and our eyes behold the vesper light,
we sing your praises, O God: Father, Son, and Holy Spirit.†

Psalm 22:18–27

Be not far away, O LORD; * you are my strength; hasten to help me.
Save me from the sword, * my life from the power of the dog.
Save me from the lion's mouth, * my wretched body from the horns of wild bulls.
I will declare your Name to my brethren; * in the midst of the congregation I will praise you.
Praise the LORD, you that fear him; * stand in awe of him, O offspring of Israel; all you of Jacob's line, give glory.
For he does not despise nor abhor the poor in their poverty; neither does he hide his face from them; * but when they cry to him he hears them.
My praise is of him in the great assembly; * I will perform my vows in the presence of those who worship him.
The poor shall eat and be satisfied, and those who seek the LORD shall praise him: * "May your heart live for ever!"
All the ends of the earth shall remember and turn to the LORD, * and all the families of

the nations shall bow before him.
For kingship belongs to the LORD; * he rules over the nations.
Glory to the Father, and to the Son, and to the Holy Spirit: * as it was in the beginning, is now, and will be for ever. Amen.

The Word

On the evening of that first day of the week, when the disciples were together, with the doors locked for fear of the Jews, Jesus came and stood among them and said, "Peace be with you!" After he said this, he showed them his hands and side. The disciples were overjoyed when they saw the Lord. Again Jesus said, "Peace be with you! As the Father has sent me, I am sending you." And with that he breathed on them and said, "Receive the Holy Spirit."
JOHN 20:19–22 (NIV)

The Word of the Lord.

Canticle

THE SONG OF MARY, LUKE 1:46–55

My soul proclaims the greatness of the Lord, my spirit rejoices in God my Savior; * for he has looked with favor on his lowly servant.
From this day all generations will call me blessed: * the Almighty has done great

things for me, and holy is his Name.
He has mercy on those who fear him * in every generation.
He has shown the strength of his arm, * he has scattered the proud in their conceit.
He has cast down the mighty from their thrones, * and has lifted up the lowly.
He has filled the hungry with good things, * and the rich he has sent away empty.
He has come to the help of his servant Israel, * for he has remembered his promise of mercy,
The promise he made to our fathers, * to Abraham and his children for ever.
Glory to the Father, and to the Son, and to the Holy Spirit: * as it was in the beginning, is now, and will be for ever. Amen.

The Apostles' Creed

I believe in God, the Father almighty,
creator of heaven and earth.
I believe in Jesus Christ, his only Son, our Lord.
He was conceived by the power of the Holy Spirit
and born of the Virgin Mary.
He suffered under Pontius Pilate,
was crucified, died, and was buried.
He descended to the dead.
On the third day he rose again.
He ascended into heaven,

and is seated at the right hand of the Father.
He will come again to judge the living and the dead.
I believe in the Holy Spirit,
the holy catholic Church,
the communion of saints,
the forgiveness of sins,
the resurrection of the body,
and the life everlasting. Amen.

The Prayers

The Lord be with you.
And also with you.
Let us pray.

Our Father in heaven,
hallowed be your Name,
your kingdom come,
your will be done,
on earth as in heaven.
Give us today our daily bread.
Forgive us our sins
as we forgive those
who sin against us.
Save us from the time of trial,
and deliver us from evil.
For the kingdom, the power,
and the glory are yours,
now and for ever. Amen.

The Petition

Show us your mercy, O Lord; * And grant us your salvation.
Clothe your ministers with righteousness; * Let your people sing with joy.
Give peace, O Lord, in all the world; * For only in you can we live in safety.
Lord, keep this nation under your care; * And guide us in the way of justice and truth.
Let your way be known upon earth; * Your saving health among all nations.
Let not the needy, O Lord, be forgotten; * Nor the hope of the poor be taken away.
Create in us clean hearts, O God; * And sustain us with your Holy Spirit.

The Collect

God of all, we pray to you for *N.*, and for all those whom we love but see no longer. Grant to them your peace; let light perpetual shine upon them; and, in your loving wisdom and almighty power, work in them the good purpose of your perfect will, through Jesus Christ our Lord. Amen.†

The Meditation

This may be read aloud by one person and followed by silence, or read by all present silently.

Jesus Christ is the same yesterday and today and forever.

HEBREWS 13:8 (NIV)

Free intercessions and/or reflections may be offered.

The Reflection

What do you hear Jesus saying to you? In what ways does Jesus appear to you? What about your loved one? Jesus may be the same always, but in what ways are you different in grief? In what ways are you unchanged?

The Conclusion

Let us bless the Lord.
  Thanks be to God.

May the God of hope fill you with all joy and peace in believing . . . through the power of the Holy Spirit. Amen.
ROMANS 15:13 (NRSV)

Friday Compline

The Invitation to Worship

The Lord Almighty grant us a peaceful night
  and a perfect end. Amen.

Answer me when I call, O God, defender of
  my cause; * you set me free when I am
  hard-pressed; have mercy on me and hear
  my prayer.
Glory to the Father, and to the Son, and to the
  Holy Spirit: * as it was in the beginning, is
  now, and will be for ever. Amen.

Psalm 22:26–30

All the ends of the earth shall remember and turn to the LORD, * and all the families of the nations shall bow before him.
For kingship belongs to the LORD; * he rules over the nations.
To him alone all who sleep in the earth bow down in worship; * all who go down to the dust fall before him.
My soul shall live for him; my descendants shall serve him; * they shall be known as the LORD's for ever.
They shall come and make known to a people yet unborn * the saving deeds that he has done.
Glory to the Father, and to the Son, and to the Holy Spirit: * as it was in the beginning, is now, and will be for ever. Amen.

The Word

Listen, I tell you a mystery: We will not all sleep, but we will all be changed—in a flash, in the twinkling of an eye. . . . For the perishable must clothe itself with the imperishable, and the mortal with immortality. When the perishable has been clothed with the imperishable, and the mortal with immortality, then the saying that is written will come true:

"Death has been swallowed up in victory."
Where, O death, is your victory?
Where, O death, is your sting?"

But thanks be to God! He gives us the victory through our Lord Jesus Christ.
I CORINTHIANS 15:51–55, 57 (NIV)

Thanks be to God.

The Meditation

This may be read aloud by one person and followed by silence, or read by all present silently.

We hide death as if it were shameful and dirty. We see in it only horror, meaninglessness, useless struggle and suffering, and intolerable scandal—whereas it is our life's culmination, its crowning moment, and what gives it both sense and worth.[19]

MARIE DE HENNEZEL

The Prayers

Into your hands, O Lord, we commend our spirits; * For you have redeemed us, O Lord, O God of truth.
Keep us, O Lord, as the apple of your eye; * Hide us under the shadow of your wings.†

Lord, have mercy.
Christ, have mercy.
Lord, have mercy.

Our Father in heaven,
hallowed be your Name,

your kingdom come,
your will be done,
on earth as in heaven.
Give us today our daily bread.
Forgive us our sins
as we forgive those
who sin against us.
Save us from the time of trial,
and deliver us from evil.

Lord, hear our prayer;
And let our cry come to you.
Let us pray.

Keep watch, dear Lord, with those who work, or watch, or weep this night, and give your angels charge over those who sleep. Tend the sick, Lord Christ; give rest to the weary, bless the dying, soothe the suffering, pity the afflicted, shield the joyous; and all for your love's sake. Amen.

Free intercessions and/or reflections may be offered.

The Reflection

How do you think the death of Christ brings meaning to your life? Can you imagine what it is like for your loved one to be living in an immortal body?

The Conclusion

Lord, you now have set your servant free * to
go in peace as you have promised;
For these eyes of mine have seen the Savior, *
whom you have prepared for all the world
to see:
A Light to enlighten the nations, * and the glory
of your people Israel.
Glory to the Father, and to the Son, and to the
Holy Spirit: * as it was in the beginning, is
now, and will be for ever. Amen.

Guide us waking, O Lord, and guard us sleeping; that awake we may watch with Christ, and asleep we may rest in peace.

Let us bless the Lord.
Thanks be to God.

The almighty and merciful Lord, Father, Son, and Holy Spirit, bless us and keep us.

Thoughts & Memories

Saturday

Saturday Morning Prayer

The Invitation to Worship

Out of the deep have I called unto thee, O Lord: * Lord, hear my voice.
The Lord is full of compassion and mercy: * Come, let us adore him.
Glory to the Father, and to the Son, and to the Holy Spirit: * as it was in the beginning, is now, and will be for ever. Amen.

Psalm 71:1–8

In you, O LORD, have I taken refuge; * let me never be ashamed.
In your righteousness, deliver me and set me free; * incline your ear to me and save me.
Be my strong rock, a castle to keep me safe; * you are my crag and my stronghold.
Deliver me, my God, from the hand of the wicked, * from the clutches of the evildoer and the oppressor.
For you are my hope, O Lord GOD, * my confidence since I was young.
I have been sustained by you ever since I was born; from my mother's womb you have been my strength; * my praise shall be always of you.
I have become a portent to many; * but you are my refuge and my strength.

Let my mouth be full of your praise * and your glory all the day long.

Glory to the Father, and to the Son, and to the Holy Spirit: * as it was in the beginning, is now, and will be for ever. Amen.

The Word

Therefore I tell you, do not worry about your life, what you will eat or drink, or about your body, what you will wear. Is not life more important than food, and the body more important than clothes?

Look at the birds of the air; they do not sow or reap or store away in barns, and yet your heavenly Father feeds them. Are you not much more valuable than they? Who of you by worrying can add a single hour to his life?

And why do you worry about clothes? See how the lilies of the field grow. They do not labor or spin. Yet I tell you that not even Solomon in all his splendor was dressed like one of these.

So do not worry, saying, "What shall we eat?" or "What shall we drink?" or "What shall we wear?" For your heavenly Father knows that you need them. But seek first his kingdom and his righteousness, and all these things will be given to you as well.

MATTHEW 6:25–29, 31, 32B–33 (NIV)

Thanks be to God.

Canticle

Song of the Redeemed, Revelation 15:3–4

O ruler of the universe, Lord God, great deeds are they that you have done, * surpassing human understanding.
Your ways are ways of righteousness and truth, * O King of all the ages.
Who can fail to do you homage, Lord, and sing the praises of your Name? * for you only are the Holy One.
All nations will draw near and fall down before you, * because your just and holy works have been revealed.
Glory to the Father, and to the Son, and to the Holy Spirit: * as it was in the beginning, is now, and will be for ever. Amen.

The Apostles' Creed

I believe in God, the Father almighty,
creator of heaven and earth.
I believe in Jesus Christ, his only Son, our Lord.
He was conceived by the power of the Holy Spirit
and born of the Virgin Mary.
He suffered under Pontius Pilate,
was crucified, died, and was buried.
He descended to the dead.
On the third day he rose again.
He ascended into heaven,

and is seated at the right hand of the Father.
He will come again to judge the living and the dead.
I believe in the Holy Spirit,
the holy catholic Church,
the communion of saints,
the forgiveness of sins,
the resurrection of the body,
and the life everlasting. Amen.

The Prayers

The Lord be with you.
And also with you.
Let us pray.

Our Father in heaven,
hallowed be your Name,
your kingdom come,
your will be done,
on earth as in heaven.
Give us today our daily bread.
Forgive us our sins
as we forgive those
who sin against us.
Save us from the time of trial,
and deliver us from evil.
For the kingdom, the power,
and the glory are yours,
now and for ever. Amen.

Save your people, Lord, and bless your inheritance; * Govern and uphold them, now and always.
Day by day we bless you; * We praise your Name for ever.
Lord, keep us from all sin today; * Have mercy on us, Lord, have mercy.
Lord, show us your love and mercy; * For we put our trust in you.
In you, Lord, is our hope; * And we shall never hope in vain.

For our *brother/sister N.*, let us pray to our Lord Jesus Christ who said, "I am Resurrection, and I am Life."

Lord, you consoled Martha and Mary in their distress; draw near to us who mourn for *N.*, and dry the tears of those who weep.

Hear us, Lord.

You wept at the grave of Lazarus, your friend; comfort us in our sorrow.

Hear us, Lord.

You raised the dead to life; give to our *brother/sister* eternal life.

Hear us, Lord.

You promised paradise to the thief who repented; bring our *sister/brother* to the joys of heaven.

Hear us, Lord.

Our *brother/sister* was washed in Baptism and anointed with the Holy Spirit; give *him/her* fellowship with all your saints.

Hear us, Lord.

S/he was nourished with your Body and Blood; grant *her/him* a place at the table in your heavenly kingdom.

Hear us, Lord.

Comfort us in our sorrows at the death of *N.*; let our faith be our consolation, and eternal life our hope.†

Silence may follow.

The Collect

Grant, O Lord, to all who are bereaved the spirit of faith and courage, that we may have strength to meet the day to come with steadfastness and patience; not sorrowing without hope, but in remembrance of your great goodness, and in the expectation of eternal life with those we love. And this we ask in the Name of Jesus Christ our Savior. Amen.†

The Meditation

This may be read aloud by one person and followed by silence, or read by all present silently.

"On Anxiety About the Future"

The future is in God's hands, not yours. God will rule it, according to your need. But if you seek to forecast it in your own wisdom, you will gain nothing but anxiety and anticipation of inevitable trouble. Try only to make use of each day. Each day brings its own good and evil, and sometimes what seems evil becomes good if we leave it to God and do not forestall him with our impatience.[20]

François Fénelon

Free intercessions and/or reflections may be offered.

The Reflection

Jesus points us toward the "lilies of the field" when we feel anxious. What are images that reduce your anxiety? What images help you "make use of each day"?

The Conclusion

Let us bless the Lord.
Thanks be to God.

Keep alert, stand firm in your faith, be courageous, be strong. Let all that you do be done in love. Amen.

I Corinthians 16:13–14 (NRSV)

The Invitation to Worship

Take courage, my children, cry to God. * And he will deliver you from the power and hand of the enemy.
Glory to the Father, and to the Son, and to the Holy Spirit: * as it was in the beginning, is now, and will be for ever. Amen.

Psalm 90:1–6, 10, 12

Lord, you have been our refuge * from one generation to another.
Before the mountains were brought forth, or the land and the earth were born, * from age to age you are God.
You turn us back to the dust and say, * "Go back, O child of earth."
For a thousand years in your sight are like yesterday when it is past * and like a watch in the night.
You sweep us away like a dream; * we fade away suddenly like the grass.
In the morning it is green and flourishes; * in the evening it is dried up and withered.
The span of our life is seventy years, perhaps in strength even eighty; * yet the sum of them is but labor and sorrow, for they pass away quickly and we are gone.

So teach us to number our days * that we may
apply our hearts to wisdom.
Glory to the Father, and to the Son, and to the
Holy Spirit: * as it was in the beginning, is
now, and will be for ever. Amen.

The Word

People were bringing little children to him, for him to touch them. The disciples scolded them, but when Jesus saw this he was indignant and said to them, "Let the little children come to me; do not stop them; for it is to such as these that the kingdom of God belongs. In truth I tell you, anyone who does not welcome the kingdom of God like a little child will never enter it." Then he embraced them, laid his hands on them and gave them his blessing.
MARK 10:13–16 (NJB)

Thanks be to God.

The Meditation
This may be read aloud by one person and followed by silence, or read by all present silently.

Some of my richest experiences have come out of my most painful times … those that were the hardest to believe would ever turn into anything positive.[21]
FRED ROGERS

The Prayers

Lord, have mercy.
  Christ, have mercy.
Lord, have mercy.

Our Father in heaven,
  hallowed be your Name,
  your kingdom come,
  your will be done,
  on earth as in heaven.
Give us today our daily bread.
Forgive us our sins
  as we forgive those
  who sin against us.
Save us from the time of trial,
  and deliver us from evil.
For the kingdom, the power,
  and the glory are yours,
  now and for ever. Amen.

The Collect

O God of grace and glory, *we* remember before you this day *our* brother (sister) *N*. We thank you for giving *her/him* to *us*, to know and to love as a companion on *our* earthly pilgrimage. In your boundless compassion, console *us* who mourn. Give us faith to see in death the gate of eternal life, so that in quiet confidence *we* may continue *our* course on earth, until, by your call, *we* are reunited with those who have gone before; through Jesus Christ our Lord. Amen.†

Free intercessions and/or reflections may be offered.

The Reflection

Some die so young, and others so old; some suffer with long disease, while others die unexpectedly. How is your grief making you more a child of God? What is your grief teaching you about what makes a life complete?

The Conclusion

Let us bless the Lord.
Thanks be to God.

Rest eternal grant to *N.*, O Lord,
And let light perpetual shine upon *him/her.*

Saturday Evening Prayer

The Invitation to Worship

I am the Resurrection, and I am the Life, says the Lord, * Whoever has faith in me shall have life, even though he die.
For if we have life, we are alive in the Lord, * And if we die, we die in the Lord.
So, then, whether we live or die, * We are the Lord's possession.

O Gracious Light

O gracious Light,
pure brightness of the everliving Father in heaven,
O Jesus Christ, holy and blessed!
Now as we come to the setting of the sun,
and our eyes behold the vesper light,
we sing your praises, O God: Father, Son, and Holy Spirit.†

Psalm 130

Out of the depths have I called to you, O LORD; LORD, hear my voice; * let your ears consider well the voice of my supplication.
If you, LORD, were to note what is done amiss, * O Lord, who could stand?
For there is forgiveness with you; * therefore you shall be feared.
I wait for the LORD; my soul waits for him; * in his word is my hope.
My soul waits for the LORD, more than watchmen for the morning, * more than watchmen for the morning.
O Israel, wait for the LORD, * for with the LORD there is mercy;
With him there is plenteous redemption, * and he shall redeem Israel from all their sins.
Glory to the Father, and to the Son, and to the Holy Spirit: * as it was in the beginning, is now, and will be for ever. Amen.

On arriving, Jesus found that Lazarus had been in the tomb for four days already. Bethany is only about two miles from Jerusalem, and many Jews had come to Martha and Mary to comfort them about their brother. When Martha heard that Jesus was coming, she went to meet him. Mary remained sitting in the house. Martha said to Jesus, "Lord, if you had been here, my brother would not have died, but even now I know that God will grant you whatever you ask of him." Jesus said to her, "Your brother will rise again." Martha said to him, "I know he will rise again at the resurrection on the last day." Jesus said: "I am the resurrection. Anyone who believes in me, even though that person dies, will live, and whoever lives and believes in me will never die. Do you believe this?" "Yes, Lord," she said, "I believe that you are the Christ, the Son of God, the one who was to come into this world."

When she had said this, she went and called her sister Mary, saying in a low voice, "The Master is here and wants to see you." Hearing this, Mary got up quickly and went to him. Jesus had not yet come into the village; he was still at the place where Martha had met him. When the Jews who were in the house comforting Mary saw her get up so quickly and go out, they followed her, thinking that she was going to the tomb to weep there. Mary went to Jesus, and as soon as she saw him she threw herself at his feet, saying, "Lord, if you had been here, my brother would not have died." At the sight of her tears, and at those of the Jews who had come with her, Jesus was greatly distressed.

JOHN 11:17–33 (NJB)

The Word of the Lord.

Canticle

THE SONG OF MARY, LUKE 1:46–55

My soul proclaims the greatness of the Lord,
my spirit rejoices in God my Savior; * for he has looked with favor on his lowly servant.
From this day all generations will call me blessed: * the Almighty has done great things for me, and holy is his Name.
He has mercy on those who fear him * in every generation.
He has shown the strength of his arm, * he has scattered the proud in their conceit.
He has cast down the mighty from their thrones, * and has lifted up the lowly.
He has filled the hungry with good things, * and the rich he has sent away empty.
He has come to the help of his servant Israel, * for he has remembered his promise of mercy,
The promise he made to our fathers, * to Abraham and his children for ever.

Glory to the Father, and to the Son, and to the Holy Spirit: * as it was in the beginning, is now, and will be for ever. Amen.

The Apostles' Creed

I believe in God, the Father almighty,
creator of heaven and earth.
I believe in Jesus Christ, his only Son, our Lord.
He was conceived by the power of the Holy Spirit
and born of the Virgin Mary.
He suffered under Pontius Pilate,
was crucified, died, and was buried.
He descended to the dead.
On the third day he rose again.
He ascended into heaven,
and is seated at the right hand of the Father.
He will come again to judge the living and the dead.
I believe in the Holy Spirit,
the holy catholic Church,
the communion of saints,
the forgiveness of sins,
the resurrection of the body,
and the life everlasting. Amen.

The Prayers

The Lord be with you
And also with you.
Let us pray.

friends? To have been someone not mentioned, such as the mother of Martha, Mary, and Lazarus?

The Conclusion

Let us bless the Lord.
Thanks be to God.

May the God of hope fill you with all joy and peace in believing . . . through the power of the Holy Spirit. Amen.
ROMANS 15:13 (NRSV)

Saturday Compline

The Invitation to Worship

The Lord Almighty grant us a peaceful night and a perfect end. Amen.

Answer me when I call, O God, defender of my cause; * you set me free when I am hard-pressed; have mercy on me and hear my prayer.
Glory to the Father, and to the Son, and to the Holy Spirit: * as it was in the beginning, is now, and will be for ever. Amen.

Psalm 77

I will cry aloud to God; * I will cry aloud, and
he will hear me.
In the day of my trouble I sought the Lord; *
my hands were stretched out by night and
did not tire; I refused to be comforted.
I think of God, I am restless, * I ponder, and
my spirit faints.
You will not let my eyelids close; * I am troubled and I cannot speak.
I consider the days of old; * I remember the
years long past;
I commune with my heart in the night; * I ponder and search my mind.
Will the Lord cast me off for ever? * will he no
more show his favor?
Has his loving-kindness come to an end for
ever? * has his promise failed for evermore?
Has God forgotten to be gracious? * has he, in
his anger, withheld his compassion?
And I said, "My grief is this: * the right hand of
the Most High has lost its power."
I will remember the works of the LORD, * and
call to mind your wonders of old time.
I will meditate on all your acts * and ponder
your mighty deeds.
Your way, O God, is holy; * who is so great a
god as our God?
You are the God who works wonders * and
have declared your power among the peoples.

By your strength you have redeemed your people, * the children of Jacob and Joseph.
The waters saw you, O God; the waters saw you and trembled; * the very depths were shaken.
The clouds poured out water; the skies thundered; * your arrows flashed to and fro;
The sound of your thunder was in the whirlwind; your lightnings lit up the world; * the earth trembled and shook.
Your way was in the sea, and your paths in the great waters, * yet your footsteps were not seen.
You led your people like a flock * by the hand of Moses and Aaron.
Glory to the Father, and to the Son, and to the Holy Spirit: * as it was in the beginning, is now, and will be for ever. Amen.

The Word

In the beginning was the Word, and the Word was with God, and the Word was God.
He was in the beginning with God. All things came into being through him, and without him not one thing came into being. What has come into being in him was life, and the life was the light of all people. The light shines in the darkness, and the darkness did not overcome it.
JOHN 1:1–5 (NRSV)

Thanks be to God.

The Meditation

This may be read aloud by one person and followed by silence, or read by all present silently.

O dying souls,
behold your living spring;
O dazzled eyes,
behold your sun of grace;
Dull ears, attend what
word this Word doth bring;
Up, heavy hearts,
with joy your joy embrace.
From death, from dark,
from deafness, from despairs,
This life, this light,
this Word,
this joy repairs.[23]

ROBERT SOUTHWELL—MODERNIZED

The Prayers

Into your hands, O Lord, we commend our spirits; * For you have redeemed us, O Lord, O God of truth.

Keep us, O Lord, as the apple of your eye; * Hide us under the shadow of your wings.†

Lord, have mercy.
Christ, have mercy.
Lord, have mercy.

Our Father in heaven,
hallowed be your Name,

your kingdom come,
your will be done,
on earth as in heaven.
Give us today our daily bread.
Forgive us our sins
as we forgive those
who sin against us.
Save us from the time of trial,
and deliver us from evil.

Lord, hear our prayer;
And let our cry come to you.
Let us pray.

Keep watch, dear Lord, with those who work, or watch, or weep this night, and give your angels charge over those who sleep. Tend the sick, Lord Christ; give rest to the weary, bless the dying, soothe the suffering, pity the afflicted, shield the joyous; and all for your love's sake. Amen.

Free intercessions and/or reflections may be offered.

The Reflection

What words of your loved one are you remembering tonight? Which of these words help you sleep? One way to think of Jesus as the Word is to think of Jesus as the one who breathed into your loved one the kindest, most loving, and life-giving words your loved one ever spoke to you.

Lord, you now have set your servant free * to
go in peace as you have promised;
For these eyes of mine have seen the Savior, *
whom you have prepared for all the world
to see:
A Light to enlighten the nations, * and the
glory of your people Israel.
Glory to the Father, and to the Son, and to the
Holy Spirit: * as it was in the beginning, is
now, and will be for ever. Amen.

Guide us waking, O Lord, and guard us sleeping; that awake we may watch with Christ, and asleep we may rest in peace.

Let us bless the Lord.
Thanks be to God.

The almighty and merciful Lord, Father, Son, and Holy Spirit, bless us and keep us.

Thoughts & Memories

Sunday

Sunday Morning Prayer

The Invitation to Worship

Out of the deep have I called unto thee, O Lord: * Lord, hear my voice.
The Lord is full of compassion and mercy: * Come, let us adore him.
Glory to the Father, and to the Son, and to the Holy Spirit: * as it was in the beginning, is now, and will be for ever. Amen.

Psalm 62:1–9

For God alone my soul in silence waits; * from him comes my salvation.
He alone is my rock and my salvation, * my stronghold, so that I shall not be greatly shaken.
How long will you assail me to crush me, all of you together, * as if you were a leaning fence, a toppling wall?
They seek only to bring me down from my place of honor; * lies are their chief delight.
They bless with their lips, * but in their hearts they curse.
For God alone my soul in silence waits; * truly, my hope is in him.
He alone is my rock and my salvation, * my stronghold, so that I shall not be shaken.
In God is my safety and my honor; * God is my strong rock and my refuge.

Put your trust in him always, O people, * pour out your hearts before him, for God is our refuge.
Glory to the Father, and to the Son, and to the Holy Spirit: * as it was in the beginning, is now, and will be for ever. Amen.

The Word

After the Sabbath, and towards dawn on the first day of the week, Mary of Magdala and the other Mary went to visit the sepulchre.

And suddenly there was a violent earthquake, for an angel of the Lord, descending from heaven, came and rolled away the stone and sat on it. His face was like lightning, his robe white as snow. The guards were so shaken by fear of him that they were like dead men.

But the angel spoke; and he said to the women: "There is no need for you to be afraid. I know you are looking for Jesus, who was crucified. He is not here; for he has risen, as he said he would. Come and see the place where he lay, then go quickly and tell his disciples, 'He has risen from the dead and now he is going ahead of you to Galilee; that is where you will see him. Look! I have told you.'"

Filled with awe and great joy the women came quickly away from the tomb and ran to tell his disciples. And suddenly, coming to meet them, was Jesus. "Greetings," he said. And the women came up to him and, clasping his feet, they did him homage.

MATTHEW 28:1–9 (NJB)

Thanks be to God.

Canticle

THE SONG OF ZECHARIAH, LUKE 1:68–79

Blessed be the Lord, the God of Israel; * he
has come to his people and set them free.
He has raised up for us a mighty savior, * born
of the house of his servant David.
Through his holy prophets he promised of old
that he would save us from our enemies, *
from the hands of all who hate us.
He promised to show mercy to our fathers *
and to remember his holy covenant.
This was the oath he swore to our father
Abraham, * to set us free from the hands of
our enemies,
Free to worship him without fear, * holy and
righteous in his sight all the days of our life.
You, my child, shall be called the prophet of
the Most High, * for you will go before the
Lord to prepare his way,
To give his people knowledge of salvation * by
the forgiveness of their sins.
In the tender compassion of our God * the
dawn from on high shall break upon us,

To shine on those who dwell in darkness and the shadow of death, * and to guide our feet into the way of peace.
Glory to the Father, and to the Son, and to the Holy Spirit: * as it was in the beginning, is now, and will be for ever. Amen.

The Apostles' Creed

I believe in God, the Father almighty,
creator of heaven and earth.
I believe in Jesus Christ, his only Son, our Lord.
He was conceived by the power of the Holy Spirit
and born of the Virgin Mary.
He suffered under Pontius Pilate,
was crucified, died, and was buried.
He descended to the dead.
On the third day he rose again.
He ascended into heaven,
and is seated at the right hand of the Father.
He will come again to judge the living and the dead.
I believe in the Holy Spirit,
the holy catholic Church,
the communion of saints,
the forgiveness of sins,
the resurrection of the body,
and the life everlasting. Amen.

The Lord be with you.
  And also with you.
Let us pray.

Our Father in heaven,
  hallowed be your Name,
  your kingdom come,
  your will be done,
  on earth as in heaven.
Give us today our daily bread.
Forgive us our sins
  as we forgive those
  who sin against us.
Save us from the time of trial,
  and deliver us from evil.
For the kingdom, the power,
  and the glory are yours,
  now and for ever. Amen.

The Petitions

Show us your mercy, O Lord; * And grant us your salvation.
Clothe your ministers with righteousness; * Let your people sing with joy.
Give peace, O Lord, in all the world; * For only in you can we live in safety.
Lord, keep this nation under your care; * And guide us in the way of justice and truth.

Let your way be known upon earth; * Your saving health among all nations.
Let not the needy, O Lord, be forgotten; * Nor the hope of the poor be taken away.
Create in us clean hearts, O God; * And sustain us with your Holy Spirit.

For our *brother/sister N.*, let us pray to our Lord Jesus Christ who said, "I am Resurrection, and I am Life."

Lord, you consoled Martha and Mary in their distress; draw near to us who mourn for *N.*, and dry the tears of those who weep.

Hear us, Lord.

You wept at the grave of Lazarus, your friend; comfort us in our sorrow.

Hear us, Lord.

You raised the dead to life; give to our *brother/sister* eternal life.

Hear us, Lord.

You promised paradise to the thief who repented; bring our *sister/brother* to the joys of heaven.

Hear us, Lord.

Our *brother/sister* was washed in Baptism and anointed with the Holy Spirit; give *him/her* fellowship with all your saints.

Hear us, Lord.

S/he was nourished with your Body and Blood; grant *her/him* a place at the table in your heavenly kingdom.

Hear us, Lord.

Comfort us in our sorrows at the death of *N.*; let our faith be our consolation, and eternal life our hope.†

Silence may follow.

The Collect

Grant, O Lord, to all who are bereaved the spirit of faith and courage, that *we* may have strength to meet the day to come with steadfastness and patience; not sorrowing without hope, but in remembrance of your great goodness, and in the expectation of eternal life with those *we* love. And this *we* ask in the Name of Jesus Christ our Savior. Amen.†

The Meditation

This may be read aloud by one person and followed by silence, or read by all present silently.

"After great pain"

After great pain, a formal feeling comes—
The Nerves sit ceremonious, like Tombs—
The stiff Heart questions was it He, that bore,

And Yesterday, or Centuries before?
The Feet, mechanical, go round—
Of Ground, or Air, or Ought
A Wooden way
Regardless grown,
A Quartz contentment, like a stone—

This is the Hour of Lead—
Remembered, if outlived,
As Freezing persons recollect the Snow—
First Chill—then Stupor—then the letting go—[24]

EMILY DICKINSON

Free intercessions and/or reflections may be offered.

The Reflection

Are there any elements of waiting in your grief? For what do you wait? How do you feel when you are waiting—silent, like this morning's psalmist? Frozen—like Emily Dickinson? What do you think the waiting was like for the Marys and Jesus' other followers? How do you imagine the risen Christ? Your risen loved one?

The Conclusion

Let us bless the Lord.
Thanks be to God.

Keep alert, stand firm in your faith, be courageous, be strong. Let all that you do be done in love. Amen.

I CORINTHIANS 16:13–14 (NRSV)

Sunday Noonday Prayer

The Invitation to Worship

Take courage, my children, cry to God. * And he will deliver you from the power and hand of the enemy.
Glory to the Father, and to the Son, and to the Holy Spirit: * as it was in the beginning, is now, and will be for ever. Amen.

Psalm 6:2–4, 6–9

Have pity on me, LORD, for I am weak; * heal me, LORD, for my bones are racked.
My spirit shakes with terror; * how long, O LORD, how long?
Turn, O LORD, and deliver me; * save me for your mercy's sake.
I grow weary because of my groaning; * every night I drench my bed and flood my couch with tears.
My eyes are wasted with grief * and worn away because of all my enemies.
Depart from me, all evildoers, * for the LORD has heard the sound of my weeping.
The LORD has heard my supplication; * the LORD accepts my prayer.

The Word

Thus says the LORD:
A voice is heard in Ramah,
lamentation and bitter weeping.
Rachel is weeping for her children;
she refuses to be comforted for her children,
because they are no more.

My joy is gone, grief is upon me,
my heart is sick.
Hark, the cry of my poor people
from far and wide in the land:
"Is the LORD not in Zion?
Is her King not in her? . . .
The harvest is past,
the summer is ended,
and we are not saved."
For the hurt of my poor people I am hurt,
I mourn, and dismay has taken hold of me.
Is there no balm in Gilead?
Is there no physician there?
Why then has the health of my poor people
not been restored?
O that my head were a spring of water,
and my eyes a fountain of tears,
so that I might weep day and night
for the slain of my poor people!

Blessed are those who trust in the LORD,
whose trust is the LORD.
They shall be like a tree planted by water,

sending out its roots by the stream.
It shall not fear when heat comes,
and its leaves shall stay green;
in the year of drought it is not anxious,
and it does not cease to bear fruit.
JEREMIAH 31:15, 8:18–9:1, 17:7–8 (NRSV)

The Word of the Lord.

The Meditation
This may be read aloud by one person and followed by silence, or read by all present silently.

How much there is to learn of love, that feeling of the body and the soul, that teaches us what God is, that He is love.[25]
DOROTHY DAY

The Prayers

Lord, have mercy.
Christ, have mercy.
Lord, have mercy.

Our Father in heaven,
hallowed be your Name,
your kingdom come,
your will be done,
on earth as in heaven.
Give us today our daily bread.
Forgive us our sins
as we forgive those
who sin against us.

Save us from the time of trial,
and deliver us from evil.
For the kingdom, the power,
and the glory are yours,
now and for ever. Amen.

The Collect

O God of grace and glory, *we* remember before you this day *our* brother (sister) *N.* We thank you for giving *her/him* to *us,* to know and to love as a companion on *our* earthly pilgrimage. In your boundless compassion, console *us* who mourn. Give *us* faith to see in death the gate of eternal life, so that in quiet confidence *we* may continue *our* course on earth, until, by your call, *we* are reunited with those who have gone before; through Jesus Christ our Lord. Amen.†

Free intercessions and/or reflections may be offered.

The Reflection

In Jeremiah, the heart-sick Lord longs for enough tears to cry without ceasing. Do you believe God is mourning with you? What are you learning about God's love, about God's being love, in your grief? Do you think grief is expanding your compassion?

The Conclusion

Let us bless the Lord.
  Thanks be to God.

Rest eternal grant to *N.*, O Lord,
And let light perpetual shine upon *him/her.*

Sunday Evening Prayer

The Invitation to Worship

I am the Resurrection, and I am the Life, says
  the Lord; * Whoever has faith in me shall
  have life, even though he die.
For if we have life, we are alive in the Lord, *
  And if we die, we die in the Lord.
So, then, whether we live or die, * We are the
  Lord's possession.†

O Gracious Light

O gracious Light,
pure brightness of the everliving Father in heaven,
O Jesus Christ, holy and blessed!

Now as we come to the setting of the sun,
and our eyes behold the vesper light,
we sing your praises, O God: Father, Son, and
Holy Spirit.†

Psalm 126

When the LORD restored the fortunes of Zion,
* then were we like those who dream.
Then was our mouth filled with laughter, * and our tongue with shouts of joy.
Then they said among the nations, * "The LORD has done great things for them."
The LORD has done great things for us, * and we are glad indeed.
Restore our fortunes, O LORD, * like the watercourses of the Negev.
Those who sowed with tears * will reap with songs of joy.
Those who go out weeping, carrying the seed, * will come again with joy, shouldering their sheaves.
Glory to the Father, and to the Son, and to the Holy Spirit: * as it was in the beginning, is now, and will be for ever. Amen.

The Word

For all who are led by the Spirit of God are children of God. For you did not receive a spirit of slavery to fall back into fear, but you have received a spirit of adoption. When we cry, "Abba! Father!" it is that very Spirit bearing witness with our spirit that we are children of God, and if children, then heirs, heirs of God and joint heirs with Christ—if, in fact, we suffer with him so that we may also be glorified with him.

I consider that the sufferings of this present time are not worth comparing with the glory about to revealed to us. For the creation waits with eager longing for the revealing of the children of God.

ROMANS 8:14–18 (NJB)

Thanks be to God.

Canticle

THE SONG OF MARY, LUKE 1:46–55

My soul proclaims the greatness of the Lord,
my spirit rejoices in God my Savior; * for he has looked with favor on his lowly servant.
From this day all generations will call me blessed: * the Almighty has done great things for me, and holy is his Name.
He has mercy on those who fear him * in every generation.
He has shown the strength of his arm, * he has scattered the proud in their conceit.
He has cast down the mighty from their thrones, * and has lifted up the lowly.
He has filled the hungry with good things, * and the rich he has sent away empty.
He has come to the help of his servant Israel, * for he has remembered his promise of mercy,
The promise he made to our fathers, * to Abraham and his children for ever.

Glory to the Father, and to the Son, and to the Holy Spirit: * as it was in the beginning, is now, and will be for ever. Amen.

The Apostles' Creed

I believe in God, the Father almighty,
creator of heaven and earth.
I believe in Jesus Christ, his only Son, our Lord.
He was conceived by the power of the Holy Spirit
and born of the Virgin Mary.
He suffered under Pontius Pilate,
was crucified, died, and was buried.
He descended to the dead.
On the third day he rose again.
He ascended into heaven,
and is seated at the right hand of the Father.
He will come again to judge the living and the dead.
I believe in the Holy Spirit,
the holy catholic Church,
the communion of saints,
the forgiveness of sins,
the resurrection of the body,
and the life everlasting. Amen.

The Prayers

The Lord be with you.
And also with you.
Let us pray.

Our Father in heaven,
hallowed be your Name,
your kingdom come,
your will be done,
on earth as in heaven.
Give us today our daily bread.
Forgive us our sins
as we forgive those
who sin against us.
Save us from the time of trial,
and deliver us from evil.
For the kingdom, the power,
and the glory are yours,
now and for ever. Amen.

The Petition

Show us your mercy, O Lord; * And grant us your salvation.
Clothe your ministers with righteousness; * Let your people sing with joy.
Give peace, O Lord, in all the world; * For only in you can we live in safety.
Lord, keep this nation under your care; * And guide us in the way of justice and truth.
Let your way be known upon earth; * Your saving health among all nations.
Let not the needy, O Lord, be forgotten; * Nor the hope of the poor be taken away.
Create in us clean hearts, O God; * And sustain us with your Holy Spirit.

The Collect

God of all, *we* pray to you for *N.*, and for all those whom *we* love but see no longer. Grant to them your peace; let light perpetual shine upon them; and, in your loving wisdom and almighty power, work in them the good purpose of your perfect will, through Jesus Christ our Lord. Amen.†

The Meditation

This may be read aloud by one person and followed by silence, or read by all present silently.

Take courage, my children, call on God:
he will deliver you from tyranny,
from the clutches of your enemies;
for I look to the Eternal for your rescue,
and joy has come to me from the Holy One
at the mercy soon to reach you
from your Savior, the Eternal.
In sorrow and tears I watched you go away,
but God will give you back to me in joy and gladness for ever.

BARUCH 4:21–23 (NJB)

Free intercessions and/or reflections may be offered.

The Reflection

What do you think Paul means by the "spirit of adoption"? What would you say to Paul, to this evening's psalmist, and to the author of the Book of Baruch about their belief that our sorrow and weeping will be transformed into etemal songs of joy and gladness? How could there be a relationship between the seeds of sorrow and the sheaves of joy?

The Conclusion

Let us bless the Lord.
  Thanks be to God.

May the God of hope fill you with all joy and peace in believing . . . through the power of the Holy Spirit. Amen.
ROMANS 15:13 (NRSV)

Sunday Compline

The Invitation to Worship

The Lord Almighty grant us a peaceful night
  and a perfect end. Amen.

Answer me when I call, O God, defender of
  my cause; * you set me free when I am
  hard-pressed; have mercy on me and hear
  my prayer.
Glory to the Father, and to the Son, and to the
  Holy Spirit: * as it was in the beginning, is
  now, and will be for ever. Amen.

Psalm 107:28–31

Then they cried to the LORD in their trouble, *
and he delivered them from their distress.
He stilled the storm to a whisper * and quieted the waves of the sea.
Then were they glad because of the calm, *
and he brought them to the harbor they were bound for.
Let them give thanks to the LORD for his mercy * and the wonders he does for his children.
Glory to the Father, and to the Son, and to the Holy Spirit: * as it was in the beginning, is now, and will be for ever. Amen.

The Word

For thus said the Lord GOD, the Holy One of Israel: In returning and rest you shall be saved; in quietness and trust shall be your strength.
ISAIAH 30:15 (NRSV)

Thanks be to God.

The Meditation
This may be read aloud by one person and followed by silence, or read by all present silently.

"Keeping Calm in Difficulty"

It is a great step forward, when in times of trouble, distress, persecution and darkness, we can keep still before God. With a calm and restful heart let us wait in His presence, assured that He will give us the victory. Let earth crumble; let our plans fall to the ground; let all things give way around us—our God is steadying the Ark, so let us wait, trust and look to Him, and all will be well.[26]

HENRY FOSTER

The Prayers

Into your hands, O Lord, we commend our
spirits; * For you have redeemed us, O
Lord, O God of truth.
Keep us, O Lord, as the apple of your eye; *
Hide us under the shadow of your wings.†

Lord, have mercy.
Christ, have mercy.
Lord, have mercy.

Our Father in heaven,
hallowed be your Name,
your kingdom come,
your will be done,
on earth as in heaven.
Give us today our daily bread.
Forgive us our sins
as we forgive those
who sin against us.
Save us from the time of trial,
and deliver us from evil.

Lord, hear our prayer;
And let our cry come to you.
Let us pray.

Keep watch, dear Lord, with those who work, or watch, or weep this night, and give your angels charge over those who sleep. Tend the sick, Lord Christ; give rest to the weary, bless the dying, soothe the suffering, pity the afflicted, shield the joyous; and all for your love's sake. Amen.

Free intercessions and/or reflections may be offered.

The Reflection

Henry Foster was a nineteenth-century physician who believed that spiritual healing is the most important component of health. Accordingly, he founded a sanitarium for ministers, missionaries, and teachers in Clifton Springs, New York. The foregoing meditation is taken from one of his chapel talks.

If you could create the perfect place to fix your mind on God, what would it be like? What kind of place can you create in your mind for returning and rest?

The Conclusion

Lord, you now have set your servant free * to
go in peace as you have promised;
For these eyes of mine have seen the Savior, *

whom you have prepared for all the world to see:
A Light to enlighten the nations, * and the glory of your people Israel.
Glory to the Father, and to the Son, and to the Holy Spirit: * as it was in the beginning, is now, and will be for ever. Amen.

Guide us waking, O Lord, and guard us sleeping; that awake we may watch with Christ, and asleep we may rest in peace.

Let us bless the Lord.
Thanks be to God.

The almighty and merciful Lord, Father, Son, and Holy Spirit, bless us and keep us. Amen.

Thoughts & Memories

The Confession of Sin

If you feel that confessing sin is helpful to you, by all means include it in the Daily Offices. The Confession is traditionally said at Morning and Evening Prayer, and at Compline following the Invitation to Worship and prior to the Psalm. Below is the Confession of Sin as found in The Book of Common Prayer *(Seabury, 1979).*

Confession of Sin

The Officiant says to the people

> Dearly beloved, we have come together in the presence of Almighty God our heavenly Father, to set forth his praise, to hear his holy Word, and to ask, for ourselves and on behalf of others, those things that are necessary for our life and our salvation. And so that we may prepare ourselves in heart and mind to worship him, let us kneel in silence, and with penitent and obedient hearts confess our sins, that we may obtain forgiveness by his infinite goodness and mercy.

or this

> Let us confess our sins against God and our neighbor.

Silence may be kept.

Officiant and People together, all kneeling

Most merciful God,
we confess that we have sinned against you
in thought, word, and deed,
by what we have done,
and by what we have left undone.
We have not loved you with our whole heart;
we have not loved our neighbors as ourselves.
We are truly sorry and we humbly repent.
For the sake of your Son Jesus Christ,
have mercy on us and forgive us;
that we may delight in your will,
and walk in your ways,
to the glory of your Name. Amen.

The Priest alone stands and says

Almighty God have mercy on you, forgive you all your sins through our Lord Jesus Christ, strengthen you in all goodness, and by the power of the Holy Spirit keep you in eternal life. *Amen.*

A deacon or lay person using the preceding form remains kneeling, and substitutes "us" for "you" and "our" for "your."

Notes

1 *Praying the Hours*, Suzanne Guthrie. (Cambridge, MA: Cowley Publications, 2000), p. 3.

2 *The Divine Hours: Prayers for Summertime*, Compiled and Edited by Phyllis Tickle. (New York: Doubleday, 2000), p. ix.

3 *Morning and Evening Prayer with Selected Psalms and Readings for the Church Year*, Compiled and Edited by Howard Galley. (New York: Church Hymnal Corporation,1994).

4 "Forever," John Boyle O'Reilly.

5 *The Little Prince*, Antoine de Saint-Exupery. Translated by Katherine Wood. (Orlando, FL: Harcourt, 1943/1982), p. 70.

6 *The Imitation of Christ*, Thomas à Kempis. (Brewster, MA: Paraclete Press, 1982), p. 201.

7 *The Wisdom of Julian of Norwich* (Grand Rapids, MI: Wm. B. Eerdmans Publishing Co., 1997), p. 64.

8 *Letters and Papers from Prison*, Dietrich Bonhoeffer. Edited by Eberhard Bethge. (New York: Collier Books, 1972), p. 176.

9 *Meditations on the Heart of God*, François Fénelon. (Brewster, MA: Paraclete Press, 1997), p. 29.

10 *The Temple: The Poetry of George Herbert*, edited by Henry Carrigan. (Brewster, MA: Paraclete Press, 2001), p. 164–165.

11 *The Practice of the Presence of God*, Brother Lawrence. (Brewster, MA: Paraclete Press, 1985), p. 136.

12 *The Joy of Full Surrender*, Jean-Pierre de Caussade. (Brewster, MA: Paraclete Press, 1986), p. 168.

13 *A Grief Observed*, C. S. Lewis (New York: Bantam Books, 1976), p. 4–5.

14 *A Year of Days with the Book of Common Prayer*, Edmund Lee Browning. (New York: Ballentine Wellspring, 1997), January 7 entry.

15 "Death is Nothing at All," Henry Scott Holland (1847–1918), Canon of St. Paul's Cathedral, London.

16 *Lead, Kindly Light*, John Henry Cardinal Newman. (Brewster, MA: Paraclete Press, 1987), p. 1.

17 "For the Fallen," Laurence Binyon, in *The Oxford Book of War Poetry*, Edited by John Stallworthy. (Oxford: Oxford University Press, 1984), p. 209.

18 *The Confessions of St. Augustine*, Augustine of Hippo. (Brewster, MA: Paraclete Press, 1986), p. 175.

19 *Intimate Death: How the Dying Teach Us How to Live*, Marie de Hennezel, Translated by Carol Brown Janeway. (New York: Alfred Knopf, 1997), p. xi.

20 *The Royal Way of the Cross*, François Fénelon. (Brewster, MA: Paraclete Press, 1982), p. 27.

21 *You Are Special*, Fred Rogers. (New York: Penguin Books, 1994), p. 103.

22 *Interior Castle*, Teresa of Avila, Translated and Edited by E. Allison Peers. (New York: Image Books, Doubleday, 1961/1989), p.113.

23 "The Nativity of Christ," Robert Southwell.

24 "After Great Pain," Emily Dickinson, written in 1862.

25 *On Pilgrimage*, Dorothy Day. (Grand Rapids, MI: Wm. B. Eerdmans Publishing Co., 1997), p. 205.

26 *Life Secrets*, Henry Foster. (Brewster, MA: Paraclete Press, 1995), p. 119.

Bibliography

Recommended Prayer Books

For companions to, or independently of, For Those We Love But See No Longer: Daily Offices for Times of Grief:

George Appleton, general editor, *The Oxford Book of Prayer* (Oxford/New York: Oxford University Press, 1985). Over 1000 years of prayers, including those about death—several from faiths other than Christianity.

Companions for the Journey series (Winona, MN: St. Mary's Press, Christian Brothers Publications, 1995). Titles include *Praying with Hildegard* and *Praying with John of the Cross.*

John Carden, compiler, *A Procession of Prayers: Meditations and Prayers from Around the World* (Harrisburg, PA: Morehouse Publishing, 1998). The life of Jesus in prayers collected by an Anglican priest who has served in several cultures.

Church of the Province of New Zealand, A New Zealand Prayer Book: He Karakia Mihinare O Aotearoa (1997). Firmly within the Anglican tradition, yet distinguished by directness of language and modern, sound psychology.

Michael Counsell, compiler, *2000 Years of Prayer* (Harrisburg, PA: Morehouse Publishing, 1999). Christian prayers chosen for beauty and poignancy. Short biographies of authors enrich the prayers' meaning. In-depth bibliography.

William John Fitzgerald; foreword by Joyce Rupp, *A Contemporary Celtic Prayer Book* (Chicago: ACTA Publications, 1998). Among these Celtic prayers, ancient and modern, are those for the "thin times" of death and mourning.

Gabriel Galache, S.J., *Methods and Practices of Anthony De Mello: Praying Body and Soul* (New York: The Crossroad Publishing Company, 1997). Spiritual exercises by a Bombay-born Jesuit priest who integrates Eastern meditation with Ignatian Christianity.

Howard Galley, compiler and editor, *Morning and Evening Prayer With Selected Psalms and Readings for the Church Year* (New York: The Church Hymnal Corporation, 1994). Conveniently-sized prayer book with varied scriptural readings according to season.

Howard Galley, compiler and editor, *The Prayer Book Office* (New York: The Church Hymnal Corporation, 1994). The Book of Common Prayer plus non-scriptural readings and other devotional material intended to enrich the Daily Office.

Suzanne Guthrie, *Praying the Hours* (Cambridge, MA: Cowley Publications, 2000). Personal essays by an Episcopal priest, including those corresponding with the Divine Offices.

Philip Law, compiler; foreword by David Adam, *A Time to Pray: 365 Classic Prayers to help you through the year* (Nashville: Dimensions for Living, 1997). Every day's prayer is provocative, whether written by Christians well-known or unknown, living or long-dead.

Praying With . . . series (Grand Rapids, MI: William B. Eerdmans Publishing Company). Titles include *Praying with St. Francis* and *Praying with St. Teresa of Avila.*

Elizabeth Roberts and Elias Amidon, compilers, *Life Prayers from Around the World* (HarperSanFrancisco, 1996). Authors of prayers on death range from Euripides to Edna St. Vincent Millay.

The Book of Common Prayer and Administration of the Sacraments and Other Rites and Ceremonies of the Church Together with The Psalter According to the Use of the Episcopal Church (Church Publishing, Inc., 1979). The venerable "BCP."

Taizé, *Prayer for Each Day* (Chicago: GIA Publications, Inc., 1998). The brothers of Taizé offer practical suggestions for praying as well as services for use throughout the Church year.

Phyllis Tickle, *The Divine Hours: Prayers for Summertime: A Manual for Prayer* (New York: Doubleday, 2000). Manuals for the other seasons are planned. Excellent introduction on the history of fixed-hour prayer.

Irma Zaleski, *Living the Jesus Prayer* (New York: Novalis/Continuum, 1997). The history and technique of this ancient discipline, shared through a personal lens.

For More on the Daily Offices

Jeffrey Lee, *Opening the Prayer Book* (Cambridge, MA: Cowley Publications, 1999). Accessible guide to the history and liturgy of *The Book of Common Prayer* by an Episcopal priest.

C.W. McPherson, *Grace at This Time: Praying the Daily Office* (Harrisburg, PA: Morehouse Publishing, 1999). History, theology and uses of the Daily Offices. Clearly written by a parish priest, teacher, and poet.

Paul V. Marshall, *Prayer Book Parallels* (New York: The Church Hymnal Corporation, 1990). Scholarly documentation of the evolution of *The Book of Common Prayer* by the Episcopal bishop of Bethlehem, PA.

Leonel L. Mitchell, *Praying Shapes Believing: A Theological Commentary on the Book of Common Prayer* (Harrisburg, PA: Morehouse Publishing, 1991). Classic resource on the role of *The Book of Common Prayer* in Christian (especially Anglican) life by a retired professor of liturgy at Notre Dame.

Web Site on *The Book of Common Prayer*: www.justus.anglican.org/resources/bcp